WHAT IS PHYSICAL INTERVENTION?

INSIDE INFORMATION FROM A LEADING UK EXPERT

Mark Dawes

NFPS Ltd
The National Federation for Personal Safety

WWW.NFPS.INFO

For more information on

PHYSICAL INTERVENTION,

including becoming a Physical Intervention Instructor, go to:

www.nfps.info

FOREWORD

Many of you reading this are hopefully looking for an insight into what physical intervention is all about. Some of you will be looking at the possibility of becoming a physical restraint instructor and some of you may be researching this field for the purpose of commissioning training.

Either way, this book has been written to give you an insight into what physical intervention actually is and the legalities and liabilities in this area, which is a very important issue right now, due to the changing legal climate that we now find ourselves in and the implications and liabilities for trainers and organisations alike, if and when something goes wrong.

One objective of this book is to dispel some of the more common myths and misconceptions that exist in the field of physical intervention in an attempt to help you make a more informed decision when considering your options, and in doing this I am sure that this book will ruffle a few feathers too. However, my intention in writing this book is to provide you with information that will enable you to make better professional choices by helping you improve your knowledge and competence, whilst also helping you reduce your liability and culpability.

For example, one of the most common question is: *"Are there any 'Governing Bodies' that exist for the accreditation or ratification of physical intervention techniques, training systems or syllabus?"* and the short answer to that question is no – in spite of what you may have been led to believe or told by some sources acting in their own self-interest.

Physical intervention is also known by many other names, such as physical restraint or control and restraint. There are also numerous training organisations who have given their own names to the systems they teach in an attempt to market it to a specific industry sector.

As there are no 'Governing Bodies' or 'Government Approved or Accredited' systems of physical intervention, it means that the whole industry itself is basically unregulated.

The net effect of this is that a wide and diverse range of training providers exist that offer a wide and diverse range of services in an unregulated industry sector, and this can make the job of choosing who to qualify with and which training provider to use, a daunting task for many of you.

The overall primary aim of this book therefore, is to provide you with a competent insight into the world of physical intervention with the purpose of answering some of the most common questions that people ask.

I must add one caveat, however. I am not a professional writer. There-fore this book is not a novel or a story with a narrative aimed at providing you with an escape from reality, so I ask you to forgive any literary inconsistencies.

I am simply someone who has been involved in this field for over twenty years of my life. I am also someone who has operationally used physical intervention, and who teaches and trains front-line staff and trainers and provides advice and consultancy on the subject.

I am known for my ability to take on jobs that others do not wish to, due to the potential liabilities that exist in certain areas and I do this out of a genuine passion to provide some assistance and answers to those who feel stuck in a bad place, without proper support or guidance.

I am also passionate about supporting those people I train. To this end I have personally attended Court and Tribunals and written reports for the same, to ensure justice gets done so that good people doing a difficult job are not 'hung out to dry' and scapegoated for something that went wrong, due a failure further up the organisa-tional chain of command.

As a result, this book has been written with the sole intention of providing you with a source of factual information that has been researched to the best of my knowledge and ability. It is a compendium resource of knowledge if you like, with the primary aim of being an information resource for you, written in a factual and explanatory way to help you make better and more competent decisions, so that you may extend a proper duty of care to those you owe it to.

However, it is not an excuse for you not to do your own due diligence in this area, and I urge you, even before you begin to read on, to question everything, even in this book. Take nothing for granted and do not assume anything.

For over twenty years I have believed that there are two main factors that end up injuring or killing people and they are - complacency and conformity, that is why, early on in my professional career, I adopted one of the most important first principles of science, which is the rigorous discipline of logic. In science this means ensuring that in any investigation all assumptions should be identified and challenged.

If assumptions are not identified and challenged we become complacent, which means that we become content in our knowledge and understanding and as a result, we stop learning and stop questioning. When this occurs we start to conform to the rules that are consistent with the limit of our understanding, simply complying with practice that has become established over time. When this happens we fail to notice those changes that challenge our established model of the world and take a more defensive stance.

My sincere advice to you is this – challenge everything - become a pain in the backside! It's always worth it in the end.

What is Physical Intervention?
By Mark Dawes

ISBN: 978 0 9571280 0 2

Published in 2011 by NFPS Ltd.

Hampshire, England.
www.nfps.info

Printed in Great Britain by Bell & Bain Ltd., Glasgow

TABLE OF CONTENTS

CHAPTER ONE
WHAT IS PHYSICAL INTERVENTION?

Physical intervention, also referred to as physical restraint, can be defined as the positive application of force for the purpose of overcoming a person's resistance.

It is generally used to:

1. Prevent the actual or imminent physical assault of self or others;

2. Effect a lawful arrest or prevent a person lawfully detained from escaping; and

3. Stop or prevent serious damage to property.

Generally physical intervention is taught as an occupational skill and is used as part of a person's employed role. For example; door supervisors - who will be required to use physical intervention to control violent and aggressive members of the public; police officers who will be expected to make arrests, and care home staff - who will be expected to intervene to protect service users from harm.

Physical intervention has its roots in the control and restraint system devised by the Prison Service in the 1980's and today physical intervention is used by the police service, the NHS, mental health services, vulnerable children and adult services and elderly care homes.

The use of physical intervention however, should be the last resort in managing violent, aggressive and challenging behaviour and should form part of an overall strategy in a member of staff's toolbox. To this end, it should be combined with other skills such as breakaway and de-escalation and negotiation training and even training in human behaviour and psychology, to enable staff to understand how some service users relate to their world from within their own psychological perspective.

In addition, as physical intervention is a skill that will degrade with time, staff initially trained in physical intervention should be refreshed regularly to ensure that their skills are kept up to date and in line with current legislation and we will come onto that later on in this book.

In some cases, particularly where the risk of injury or fatality is high, staff should also be trained in first aid and, if required, the use of life monitoring and life saving equipment, such as pulse oximetors and defibulators.

RESTRICTIVE AND LEAST-RESTRICTIVE PHYSICAL INTERVENTION

Physical interventions are generally broken down into two main subcategories, which are 'Restrictive' and 'Least-Restrictive'.

A restrictive physical intervention is a term normally associated with the application of a higher level of force used to control a person's behaviour against their will. In these cases, more restrictive techniques, even the use of pain-compliance techniques are used, if required, to achieve control.

A 'least-restrictive' or 'low-level' physical intervention on the other hand, is normally associated with a technique that does not generally use a high degree of force to achieve compliance. In these situations, force is not generally applied against a person's will, so to achieve the desired outcome the person whom force is being used upon is, to a degree, 'compliant', whereas if they weren't, a more restrictive degree of force would have to be applied against their will, to achieve the same result.

Escorting, for example, would be classified as a least-restrictive or low-level intervention and escorting is defined as: *"to accompany for the purpose of protection of guidance" (Oxford English Dictionary)* and is most commonly used when supportive assistance is given to a subject who is complying with the use of physical force. In general, when we are escorting someone they are normally compliant and therefore the use of force is not generally applied without a person's consent.

Another example of a 'least-restrictive' or 'low-level' intervention would be the use of 'holding', which has been defined by the Children Act 1989 as: *"a commonly used, and often helpful containing experience for a distressed child".*

The Royal College of Nursing Guidance (Restraining, Holding Still and Containing Children: Guidance for Nursing Staff, April 2003) also provides a definition of what a holding technique may be. It states: *"It may be a method of helping children, with their permission, to manage a painful procedure quickly and effectively. Holding is distinguished from restraint by the degree of force required and the intention."*

A point to bear in mind however is that a 'holding technique' may still be used to restrain. In these situations, we could still be using force without consent. In these cases though, emphasis is normally placed on using firm grips or holds, as opposed to locks or other techniques that could intentionally cause pain.

There may also be exceptional circumstances however, when staff have no option but to use a pain-compliance technique, such as a wrist-lock for example, in order to control someone who would not be able to be controlled with a lesser degree of force. Due to the emotive and sensitive nature of this issue I have dedicated a whole chapter to the use of pain compliance techniques, which you can read about further along in this book.

OTHER FORMS OF RESTRAINT

Physical intervention is not just about the use of physical force. The Oxford English Dictionary defines the word 'restraint' as: *"To keep in check or under control or within bounds, confine, imprison."*

Therefore, if we take the literal meaning of the word 'restrain' it means more than just the use of force by one or more people, to control another.

In fact, any action that removes a person's liberty (their freedom to go about their lawful business, to do as they please, make their own choices and move about freely without restriction) is a form of restraint.

The simple locking of a door, to stop someone leaving a room of their own free will, can be defined as a form of restraint. Removing a person's ability to make independent choices about how they go about their day to day business, for example, an elderly person whose daily routine is controlled by a care home, or whose finances are administered by their family, are also examples of how we can inadvertently restrict another person's liberty, and in doing so be applying a form of restraint or restriction in their lives. It is for these reasons that other pieces of legislation and guidance, such as the Mental Capacity Act 2005 (and its associated code of practice) and the Deprivation of Liberty Safeguards Code of Practice, have come about, which have particular relevance for those people who are residing in hospitals or care homes and who may also lack the capacity to make everyday decisions.

Sometimes however, the range of legislation and guidance and approved codes of practice, all of which are intended to provide clarity, result in confusion, especially if combined with a subjective opinion of what someone thinks it means, as opposed to actually finding out what it actually means.

For example, I was once asked to provide some consultancy for a care home for the elderly. On arriving at the home I noticed that all of the locks on the door of the home had been removed making it impossible for the doors to be locked. On further investigation of this issue I was informed by the care home manager of this residential unit, that cares for people with dementia, that the local NVQ assessor had recently undertaken a visit and had informed them that all of the locks on the doors had to be removed, because they amounted to a restriction of liberty.

I asked what the effect of having no locks on the doors was having on the home and I was told that on some occasions, elderly people (with dementia) will simply open the door and walk out of the home and in some cases, this has occurred late in the evening and during the night. When this happens, staff have been told that they can follow the elderly person and try to encourage them to come back to the home, using persuasion and negotiation, but that they are not allowed to physically touch them and physically escort them back to the home because that would be a restriction of the elderly person's liberty. Staff were also told that as the elderly people in the home have human rights, it would also be infringing their human rights to restrain them against their will and if they did that they would be breaching the Mental Capacity Act 2005 Deprivation of Liberty Safeguards Code of Practice and could be liable to discipline.

The result of this was that one elderly gentleman used to walk out of the home late in the evening. This was during the month of November, which is not one of our warmest months. He would walk out dressed only in his nightclothes and with nothing on his feet. He would walk across main roads, including a dual carriageway and across a railway crossing – and yet staff were told, by the NVQ assessor, that they were not allowed to lock the doors of the home to prevent this happening, nor physically escort him back to the home if he started to wander outside. This is an elderly gentleman who suffers from dementia in a home designed to care for him!

Yet this isn't what the legislation and guidance was designed for at all. This was the net effect of someone (in this case the NVQ assessor) adding their subjective interpretation to what they 'think' the guidance means, sometimes without even reading it. How do I know this – I read everything and this is what the guidance actually says:

> *"Restraint is illegal unless it can be demonstrated that for an individual in particular circumstances not being restrained would conflict with the duty of care of the service. And that the outcome for the individual would be harm to themselves or others." (Guidance for Inspectors: How To Move Towards a Restraint Free Care)*

> *"Where people in care services have capacity restraint may only take place with their consent or in an emergency to prevent harm to themselves or others or to prevent a crime being committed." (Ibid, no,6)*

> *"Preventing a person from leaving a care home or hospital unaccompanied because there is a risk that they would try to cross a road in a dangerous way, for example, is likely to be seen as a proportionate restriction to prevent the person from coming to harm. That would be unlikely, in itself, to constitute a deprivation of liberty. Similarly, locking a door to guard against immediate harm is unlikely, in itself, to amount to a deprivation of liberty." (Mental Capacity Act, Code of Practice, 2.10)*

To summarise, we had the locks replaced and staff were given training in specifically what they could and could not do and the situation in that home was resolved.

But there is a moral to this story, and if you haven't worked it out as yet, here it is: Do not simply accept something, without question, that which you genuinely believe to be wrong. Question it, and if necessary, challenge it. In short, if you don't know, find out. It is worth the work.

CHAPTER TWO
THE CHANGING LEGAL CLIMATE

On the 16th February 2011, at Winchester Crown Court, Cotswold Geotechnical Holdings became the first company to be convicted of the offence of Corporate Manslaughter under the Corporate Manslaughter and Corporate Homicide Act 2007.

The conviction followed a lengthy trial into the death of Alex Wright, a young geologist employed by the company, who died on the 5th September 2008 when a deep trench that he was working in collapsed and killed him.

The company was found guilty of Corporate Manslaughter primarily because it failed to protect the young geologist from working in dangerous conditions that led to his death.

To find the company guilty, the Crown Prosecution Service had to establish that the way in which the senior management of Cotswold Geotechnical Holdings managed its activities formed a substantial element of the breach of the duty of care owed that led to Alex Wright's death, which they successfully did.

In convicting the company of Corporate Manslaughter, the jury came to the conclusion that the system of digging trial pits was unnecessarily dangerous and that the company had ignored well-recognised industry guidance in this area.

This was echoed during the summing up of the trial, when the prosecutor told the jury that:

> *"The substantial cause of Alex Wright's death was the failure of the company to manage its affairs so as to comply with its legal duty to ensure that Alex Wright's health was not put at risk."*

In short, Cotswold Geotechnical Holdings was found guilty of Corporate Manslaughter because:

1. It failed to protect a member of staff working in conditions known to be dangerous;

2. The company ignored well-recognised industry guidance in this area;

3. There was a gross breach of the duty of care owed to the member of staff who died, and;

4. The way in which its activities were managed or organised by its senior management formed a substantial element of the breach that led to Alex Wright's death.

In essence, the senior management of the company knew that unnecessary risks were being taken that went against good practice guidance, yet they chose to ignore it, and that ignorance resulted in a member of staff dying.

SO, HOW COULD THIS CASE AFFECT THOSE OF US WHOSE STAFF USE PHYSICAL INTERVENTION AT WORK, TEACH PHYSICAL INTERVENTION OR COMMISSION PHYSICAL INTERVENTION TRAINING?

To answer that question we simply need to ask a series of questions based on the previous case, which are:

1. Does your organisation allow staff to work in foreseeably hazardous and knowingly dangerous conditions, yet allow the situation to remain dangerous by doing nothing about it, apart from teaching them physical intervention skills as the primary way of controlling the risk without looking at alternatives?

2. Does your organisation teach staff or allow and even possibly encourage staff to be taught to physically intervene on their own, when it is well documented that single–person restraint increases the risk of harm to staff and the person being restrained?

3. Is your organisation still teaching physical intervention techniques that have the potential to increase the risk of death from positional asphyxia, like the prone position, basket-holds or the seated double-embrace technique?

4. Is your organisation failing to adequately train staff to a sufficiently competent level so that the skills they are being taught are fit for purpose?

5. Is your organisation failing to teach staff how to use physical intervention within the constraints laid down by UK statute and common law? In other words, are you failing to give your staff legally correct advice and guidance?

6. Can you evidence all of the above if required?

If you have answered yes to any of the above questions then you have a problem, if and when a death results.

PROSECUTIONS FOR DEATHS IN CUSTODY

In addition, an amendment to the Corporate Manslaughter and Corporate Homicide Act 2007, which came into effect on the 13 September 2011 means that organisations can now be prosecuted under the Corporate Manslaughter & Corporate Homicide Act, for deaths in custody.

The extension of the Corporate Manslaughter Act to now enable prosecutions of organisations for deaths in custody will add to the Crown Prosecution Service's ability to prosecute individuals (such as prison officers, nurses, doctors etc.) for individual gross negligence manslaughter and the standard health and safety offences that have always been available (and are still available) to be used against organisations.

The new amendment means that public authorities and private companies can be prosecuted under the Act if they fail to ensure the safety of someone in their care. Examples of this could include deaths during an immigration removal or when someone has been restrained using an authorised and badly taught body hold.

A positive effect of the law change is that it may provide added impetus to drive further improvements in the prison service, in care homes, and in mental health trusts to prevent suicides, fatal acts of violence between prisoners or patients themselves or involving staff, neglect of care and supervision resulting in fatal incidents and the use of known physical intervention techniques that increase the risk of death.

In considering any future prosecution under the new amendment the Crown will have to take into consideration whether or not a significant portion of that breach is related to the way in which senior management run the organisation, and also whether a death can be attributed to the neglect, consent or connivance of the organisational management.

These new changes in the law have major implications for many agencies that have custody of vulnerable individuals, especially those individuals who are likely to be more vulnerable and present a possible high risk of fatality when restrained. They also have major implications for those organisations who allow bad practice and un-safe systems of work to continue to be used or actively encouraged by neglect, consent or connivance, such as allowing staff to physi-cally restrain on their own.

SWIFTER JUSTICE FOR WORKPLACE DEATHS

In addition to the implementation of the new amendment to the Corporate Manslaughter and Corporate Homicide Act 2007, a key amendment to the Work-Related Deaths Protocol (WRDP) came into effect on the 1st October 2011, and this has changed the way work-place deaths are now to be investigated and prosecuted.

What this new amendment means is that there are now likely to be more health and safety prosecutions for deaths in the workplace pri-or to an Inquest taking place.

Prior to this amendment, cases were only taken before an Inquest by the Health and Safety Executive in exceptional circumstances and normally in connection with manslaughter related charges. Now, where manslaughter or homicide charges are not relevant, the re-vised protocol will allow a health and safety prosecution before an Inquest – if it is considered appropriate and in the interest of justice.

The changes were announced by the Work Related Deaths National Liaison Committee (NLC) and are supported by the Coroners' Society.

The NLC was set up in 1998 and its aims are to improve the communication and collaborative working between all members when involved with a work-related death. Members currently include, amongst others, the CPS, the Health and Safety Executive, the British Transport Police and Local Authorities.

Richard Daniels, Chair of the NLC, said:

> "All signatories are committed to seeking justice for bereaved family members, when a work-related death has occurred and someone should be held to account. The change will help us deliver this justice more effectively and sooner in less complex cases. The NLC has worked closely with the Coroners' Society to agree the changes and they support this swifter resolution of prosecutions in some cases. We also welcome the Maritime and Coastguard Agency and the Chief Fire Officers' Association as formal signatories of the revised protocol."

This is a very important amendment to consider for all of us who are involved with the use of physical force in the workplace, especially commissioning agencies that either actively condone or turn a blind eye to the use of known techniques that increase the risk of positional asphyxia. In short, if a restraint related death occurs due to the use of a knowingly unsafe technique, then the HSE, CPS, Police and Local Authorities can now prosecute prior to an Inquest taking place.

So just take a moment to stop and reflect - what is going to happen now if someone dies in your care? Just think for a moment how your systems, training and management will be scrutinised by the Health and Safety Executive and the Crown Prosecution Service, and try to consider how you will be able to justify what you did or did not do when cross-examined by a qualified solicitor in court.

Now, as you reflect on the above, consider this. In an attempt to reduce their liability many organisations will use training that is 'recommended' by let's say their local authority who have signed up to a particular code of practice that they believe is endorsed by some sort of Government approval, or a local education authority or council who have a contract with a particular training provider. Their aim being, to standardise training within the schools in their local area without actually considering what the training provider will teach. However, some training providers are still actively teaching some techniques that they shouldn't as primary methods of intervention, such as: prone restraint, double basket-holds, nose distraction techniques, etc., without even looking at any possible alternatives, and I do wonder how soon it is likely to be before another person dies and the head of the commissioning organisation finds themselves being prosecuted.

You see the fact is, that the head of any commissioning organisation is ultimately responsible and accountable for whatever training they allow to be taught in their organisation. For example, in schools the head-teacher of every school is ultimately responsible and accountable for whatever system of training is delivered in their school. As a result, they have to use their due diligence in finding the most appropriate specific system. This was highlighted in a letter received from a representative from the Department of Education who wrote:

> "... the Government does not endorse individual training providers, or the content of their courses and materials. A wide variety of training organisations offer their services to schools on a commercial basis, and schools now have the autonomy to make their own decisions on which service is most appropriate for them. Ministers believe that head teachers and their immediate colleagues are best placed to determine what training is appropriate for their staff".

This is the same for all organisations that commission training, and the short message is - don't be fooled by a badge of approval.

LET THE GREAT AXE FALL

On 6th June 2000 Anthony Scrivener QC was the keynote speaker at the Annual Symonds Safety Lecture at the Institution of Civil Engineers. The lecture was entitled 'Corporate and Personal Manslaughter: Where the Offence is - Let the Great Axe Fall'. His talk began with the following opening statement:

> "Although in this short address I will refer to the Government's new proposals for corporate manslaughter I would wish to drive home a clear message to all of those involved in the management of companies. Even without these reforms there is an unstoppable movement towards using the full force of the criminal law against

companies and executives forming the management of companies where death or injury is caused by serious negligence. They are out to get you and that is the clear message you should take back with you from this meeting to your boardroom. If you ignore the trend then you do so at your peril."

Anthony Scrivener QC Tuesday 6th June 2000

It is now over eleven years ago since that speech was made and the words of Mr. Scrivener QC have come true. The Corporate Manslaughter and Corporate Homicide Act received Royal Assent on 26th July 2007 and came into force on 6 April 2008, seven years and ten months to the day since that speech was made. Its aim, simply to make organisations more accountable and to be more easily brought to justice where death occurs in the workplace, and as you have already seen, it is starting to bare its teeth.

Do your own due diligence.

CHAPTER THREE
THE HUMAN RIGHTS ACT

The Human Rights Act came into effect on the 2nd October 2000 and it is the most significant statement of human rights since the 1689 Bill of Rights. It gives every citizen a clear statement of rights and responsibilities and provides for every citizen to challenge more easily actions of the state and of other such public authorities.

The United Kingdom helped draft the European Convention on Human Rights in 1950, and the 1998 Act makes this convention a part of UK law. Under the Human Rights Act it is now unlawful for a public authority to act incompatibly with the Convention rights and allows for a case to be brought to a UK Court or tribunal against the authority, if it does so. What this means is that instead of having to go to Strasbourg, people can use the UK courts to enforce their human rights. This reform is part of the modernisation of our constitution, making Government more responsible to the people ensuring that the rights of UK citizens become an everyday part of UK law.

Section 6 of the Human Rights Act 1998 now makes it unlawful for a public authority to act in a way that is incompatible with a Convention right. This means it requires all legislation, including policy, procedure and approved codes of practice, to be interpreted and given effect as far as possible compatible with the Convention rights.

In the field of physical intervention this legislation has a monumental impact on the way in which training is managed, structured and delivered, as all physical intervention training must comply with the Convention's rights if it can be considered as legal. This means that training can no longer simply be 'technique dependent' but must incorporate fully the protected rights of the individual as detailed within the Convention.

ARTICLE 2 – THE RIGHT TO LIFE

Article 2 of the Act is the primary article that we need to consider when addressing use of force contingencies within organisations. The article raises specific issues with regard to the use of physical force with regard to the right to life. In the first part of Article 2, it states,

> *"Everyone's right to life shall be protected by law. No one shall be deprived of his life intentionally save in the execution of a sentence of a court following his conviction of a crime for which this penalty is provided by law."*

This has direct implications in the way in which the activity of physical intervention is managed within organisations including ensuring that the training, the manuals and the policy and procedure, promote a positive duty to the preservation of life.

The positive duty to preserve life is even more crucial when we consider the use of physical intervention in organisations where certain individuals have little or no control over their lives. For example, people who are held in a secure institution, a care home or a prison, who may also be vulnerable and who will have very little control over the system of physical intervention used to control them.

This Article is so important that in April 2002, the Police Complaints Authority (the forerunner to the Independent Police Complaints Commission [IPCC]) issued a report entitled 'Safer Restraint', which was a report from a conference by the same name held in Westminster. The conference was attended by Chris Mullin MP (the then Chair of the Home Affairs Committee), Sir Alistair Graham (the then Chair of the Police Complaints Authority) and representatives from the Police and Prison service, as well as Forensic Medical experts and a Chief Constable, to name but a few.

The aim of the report was to learn from previous restraint related deaths and move forward towards creating a model of best practice, including making strong recommendations for preventing future deaths and for the investigation of such deaths.

In doing so, the report took into consideration the inclusion of the Human Rights Act 1998, which had become part of UK law in October 2000, only two years prior to the conference taking place. The following is the exact text taken from the report:

"THE HUMAN RIGHTS PERSPECTIVE

The Human Rights Act 1998 came fully into force in October 2000, incorporating into UK law the provisions of the European Convention on Human Rights (ECHR).

The change is of great significance when judging standards of policing and the Act creates a new mechanism – in addition to present criminal, civil and disciplinary procedures – for making individual police officers, their organisations and practices accountable. Police forces must be seen to act in ways that are lawful, necessary, proportionate and non-discriminatory.

Particularly important in the context of this report is Article 2 of the Act – the right to life, the most fundamental of all civil and political rights. It says that the state has a positive duty in law to protect the lives of everyone in its jurisdiction. It goes on to stress that any force used must be 'no more than absolutely necessary'.

The responsibility of the state in this regard is total – it is no defence against an Article 2 violation for an institution or public authority to say that the problem lay elsewhere or to 'scapegoat' individual officers. The issue is not restricted to the specific circumstances or individuals directly involved in a death – it covers also all those within an agency who are responsible for planning, preparation, training and protection as well as the government departments that oversee those agencies.

The Act requires thoroughness. In relation to restraint-related deaths, it applies to codes of practice, training courses and manuals, procedures and so on and even perceived attempts on the part of senior managers or other leaders to avoid the issue. If the state, in all or any of its manifestations, has realised that there is a problem and understood the nature of that problem but has failed to deal with it adequately, there will be a violation of Article 2 if that failure subsequently leads to a death.

The right to life is crucial and it requires us to explore alternative remedies or methods before using those that we know to be dangerous.

In other words, it is everyone's responsibility to do their utmost to protect the right to life of all those people whose lives the state has taken control over, in custody or institutions and who are more dependent on the protection of the state than most of the rest of the population."

To understand further the implications of this positive duty as required by Article 2 of the Human Rights Act, we need to refer to the controversial case of *McCann v United Kingdom (McCann v United Kingdom [1995] 21 EHRR 97)*; which involved the shooting and killing of three members of the Provisional IRA by soldiers of the Army's Special Air Service Regiment.

The key issue in this case is that the court not only looked at the decisions made and actions taken by the SAS soldiers who pulled the trigger which led to the deaths of the three members of the Provisional IRA, but also the planning and control of the actions by the State.

In the Judge's summing up of the case, he stated "in making any decision a Court will take into consideration not only the actions of staff who actually administer the force but also the surrounding circumstances including such matters as the planning and control of the actions under examination." This idea of planning and control is important. The Court held that *"the State (in the case of McCann v United Kingdom [1995] 21 EHRR 97) must give appropriate training, instructions and briefing to its agents who are faced with a situation where the use of lethal force is possible. The State must also exercise 'strict control' over any operations that may involve the use of lethal force."*

How does this case law affect public authorities? Well for 'State' substitute 'public authority' and for 'agents' substitute 'staff', and for 'planning and control' substitute 'risk assessment'.

In the McCann case, the court not only looked at the decision-making and actions by those who pulled the trigger, which led to the deaths, but at the planning process, the training and the protection offered by the State.

The violation of Article 2 came not from those who pulled the trigger but from the fact that the preparation and training was inadequate. One of the key issues was whether these individuals should have been let into Gibraltar in the first place, or whether they should have been arrested earlier?

Now, when considering this point go back to the point made earlier in relation to the Corporate Manslaughter and Corporate Homicide Act 2007 where the question was asked: "Does your organisation allow staff to work in foreseeably hazardous and knowingly dangerous conditions, yet allow the situation to remain dangerous by doing nothing about it, apart from teaching them physical intervention skills as the primary way of controlling the risk without looking at alternatives?"

Can you see the link now between the Corporate Manslaughter and Corporate Homicide Act 2007 and the Human Rights Act 1998, that we covered earlier?

Therefore, when we are considering the use of physical intervention in our workplaces, points we have to consider are:

1. If we actually know what the problem is and we fail to adequately deal with it, and that failure leads to a subsequent death, then that is a breach of Article 2 of the Human Rights Act, particularly where;

2. The death could have been prevented by the taking of positive and pro-active steps, consistent with Article 2, which requires all authorities (including some private companies) to take positive steps consistent with the positive obligation to preserve life, especially where a risk to life is evident.

With regard to the use of physical intervention therefore, the positive obligation to preserve life must be at the forefront of all of our minds when delivering physical interventions skills training and implementing use of force strategies in the workplace.

This means avoiding, unless absolutely necessary, the need to teach techniques that are known to increase the risk of death; such as prone restraints, single and double-basket holds, seated double-embrace techniques and neck holds, whilst being pro-active in using techniques and finding strategies that promote the right to life.

ARTICLE 3 - PROHIBITION OF TORTURE

Article 3 of the Human Rights Act 1998 states that:

"No one shall be subjected to torture or to inhuman or degrading treatment or punishment."

This article concerns itself with freedom from torture, inhumane treatment, degrading treatment, inhumane punishment and degrading punishment, and its provision aims to protect an individual from physical and mental ill treatment and is therefore, relevant when considering the use of physical intervention.

The Government has positive obligations under Article 3 which mean that it has a duty to investigate allegations of torture and to prevent breaches of the Article by one private individual against another, particularly against children and other vulnerable persons. As such, some care standards inspectors will be required to consider whether the system or techniques used within a physical intervention programme amount to torture, inhumane or degrading treatment or punishment.

Therefore, in addition to the strict obligation and absolute duty to promote the right to life as required by Article 2 of the Act we must also refrain from using any technique or system that amounts to an act of torture, or which subjects people to inhumane and degrading treatment and punishment as required by Article 3 of the Act.

This would, for example, obviously include the prohibition of techniques that would involve placing people who have been sexually abused face down on the floor with someone straddled across their back to hold them in that position and female prisoners handcuffed to beds when giving birth. Both of which, even if not reaching the threshold to prove that torture took place, would be very likely to fall within the scope of inhumane and degrading treatment.

If restrictive interventions are being used regularly and pain is being unnecessarily caused, particularly where a lesser restrictive or less harmful technique could be as effective, then there may be grounds for bringing an action against an employer against Article 3 for torture and / or inhumane and degrading treatment and punishment. An example could be where a service user is being accommodated in an environment that doesn't have the resources to manage him or her and staff as a result, consistently have to use high levels of intervention to prevent harm.

And this whole issue raises another important question in relation to Article 3, which is – is it legal to use a pain-compliant technique as part of a system of physical intervention?

However, what if the use of such techniques were banned, and a death occurred, which could have been prevented by the use of a pain-compliant technique? Wouldn't that amount to a breach of Article 2 – the positive obligation to preserve life?

CHAPTER FOUR
THE USE OF PAIN-COMPLIANCE TECHNIQUES

There has always been a lot of controversy regarding the use of pain-compliance techniques within physical intervention programmes and as a result quite a few myths and misconceptions have arisen regarding the use of such techniques, one obviously being that the use of a pain-compliance technique amounts to an act of torture.

I have even personally heard speakers at events, state that any technique that causes pain is a breach of Article 3 of the Human Rights Act 1998 as it would amount to an act of torture, especially if used on a vulnerable service user. This is even supported by the views of certain Government Inspectors – many not even trained in the legal aspects relating to the use of force!

BILD (the British Institute of Learning Disabilities) runs a physical intervention accreditation scheme based around its physical intervention code of practice (third edition 2010), which is opposed to the use of techniques that may cause pain, and will not accredit any organisation that uses pain-compliance techniques.

In the BILD Code of Practice (item 6.4) it states that:

> "BILD is morally and ethically opposed to the use of deliberate infliction of pain, as a means of control in the sectors of care and education covered by this guidance."

In short, if you teach or propose to use any technique that causes pain, your organisation will not be accredited by BILD. However, we will be covering more about BILD accreditation later on in this book.

The issue of pain-compliance is such a contentious issue that on the 21st March 2011, it was reported in the *Independent* newspaper that a report issued by the Children's Commissioner for England has asked for the deliberate use of pain to restrain young people in custody to be banned on the basis that it is not in the best interest of the child.

However, this absolute view is wrong and we need to take a much more sophisticated look at this issue, as opposed to the simple knee-jerk over-generalised perception promoted by many well meaning and good intentioned, yet ill informed, people who are quick to jump to the conclusion that any amount of pain caused, be it intentionally or unintentionally, is an act of torture.

The reason this needs to be addressed is that such opinions, especially from people in positions of influence, can actually lead to a serious breach of the duty of care owed, to the very vulnerable service user that they are trying to safeguard. In addition, such advice can also compromise the duty of care owed to the member of staff too, and this is why this particular issue needs to be addressed.

Now, I must stress that I am not promoting the use of pain over non-pain compliance techniques, where a non-pain compliance technique will achieve control. However, I am stressing that we act in the best interests of the service user and staff in reducing any unnecessary risk of death or serious injury, and if that means that a more restrictive technique and even a pain-compliance technique should be used to prevent a greater harm from occurring, especially where a non-pain compliance technique has, or is likely to fail, then yes, I am advocating that it should be used. Why? Because that is not only consistent with the requirements of law, including the Human Rights Act 1998, but it is also morally and ethically correct, if it is in the best interests of the service user and staff.

The dichotomy that exists is that the avoidance of such techniques, due to management or even inspectoral duress, can, in some situations, increase the risk to the service user and also staff. The operational paradox that front line staff face as a direct result of this imposed duress from above is; do they act in the best interests of the service user in protecting them from harm, or in *their* own best interest in an attempt to avoid disciplinary or criminal prosecution?

BACK TO BASIC LEGAL PRINCIPLES

In general terms, the basis for any legal decision regarding the use of force will be whether the force used was 'reasonable in the circum-stances' i.e., was the force used, honestly believed to be necessary and was the application of force proportionate to the achievement of its permitted purpose. Which generally means, did it prevent a greater level of harm from happening, when used to prevent a crime or harm to oneself or another or serious damage to property.

If you apply that basic understanding of reasonable force, you can clearly see that if a pain-compliance technique is used to prevent a greater harm from occurring then that is a lawful response. However, if the same outcome can be achieved by use of a lesser restrictive method of control then that should always be the option.

However, where a lesser or least restrictive method of control is high-ly likely to fail, or has failed, then the use of a more restrictive hold or the application of pain will have to be considered if that in itself prevents a greater harm from occurring. This would not only be good risk management, consistent with Health and Safety legislation, but where there is a risk to life then the use of such techniques is also consistent with the positive obligation to preserve life as required by Article 2(1) of the Human Rights Act.

Although not possibly 'politically correct' the use of such techniques may not only be required, but also be absolutely crucial, when con-sideration is given to the natural ability [or lack of] of staff and the ability of the service users, who staff may have to restrain.

However, many people argue the issue that the use of a pain-compli-ance technique is not ethical or moral. As ethics and morals relate to the 'goodness' or 'badness' of human conduct how can it be morally wrong and ethically incorrect to use something that with the pro-active and positive intention of preserving life and reducing harm? This was something that was raised in a recent report published in March 2011.

REPORT ON IMPLEMENTING THE INDEPENDENT REVIEW OF RESTRAINT IN JUVENILE SECURE SETTINGS

An independent report in relation to restraint in juvenile secure settings was undertaken by Peter Smallridge CBE and Andrew Williamson CBE and published in March 2011.

In Section 4 of the report, entitled, 'The Safety and Ethics of Restraint' it reports on its findings into the use of pain compliance techniques, and the following is an extract from that section:

> "When writing our original report, we (reluctantly) came
> to the conclusion that in some circumstances, pain com-
> pliance was necessary. During the two-year monitoring
> period, this conclusion has not changed. The overarching
> point of importance is based on the length of time that a
> young person is restrained. Through the drafting of our
> original report we found that the longer a young person
> is restrained the more one risks a young person's safety.
> In effect, restraint techniques that incorporate pain com-
> pliance holds are a way of quickly and safely ending the
> need for prolonged use of restraint techniques.
>
> We understand the sensitivities and controversial nature
> of this debate and this has been discussed in various
> workshops and meetings. We take the time to stress again
> that we came to this conclusion with the safety of the
> young person as the paramount concern.
>
> Although pain-compliant techniques are sometimes nec-
> essary, we believe they must be safeguarded to ensure
> protection of the young person. Our hope is that staff will
> be provided with a range of techniques and training so
> that when instances arise that require pain compliance
> techniques, they are able to do it in a way that ensures
> the safety of both the young person and staff members.
>
> During a stakeholder workshop on restraint in December
> 2010, we spoke to various interested parties who raised
> the issue of handcuffs as a powerful de-escalation tool.
> Representatives from the youth secure estate consid-
> ered handcuffs were an effective tool because they have
> 'no personality' and can be used to end swiftly a danger-
> ous situation without the use of pain."

THE 'BEST INTEREST OF THE CHILD' IS THE PARAMOUNT CONSIDERATION

Interestingly, under Children's legislation, the 'best interests of the
child' is the paramount consideration, and is the doctrine used by
all family courts to determine a wide range of issues relating to the
well being of children. The most common of these issues generally

concern questions that arise upon the divorce or separation of the children's parents.

However, this doctrine must surely extend beyond these general issues into other areas of a child's welfare when considering the wider context of how we act in the best interests of the child, and this can be achieved by adopting a more universal approach to the 'best interest criteria' as opposed to simply the more general unilateral approach.

For example, in relation to the use of force on a child - it must be in the best interest of the child to avoid any technique that we know could increase the risk of harm or possible death. This has to be a paramount consideration and must surely be consistent with the best interest of the child doctrine. If agencies were to adopt this approach then this would also be consistent with what is required by Article 2(1) of the Human Rights Act 1998 which requires that all public authorities (whether direct or quasi) take positive steps to promote and preserve the right to life - especially where a risk to life is known to exist, such as in a banned physical intervention technique for example, that has been implicated in a death of a child in a restraint.

THE HUMAN RIGHTS ACT - PROMOTING THE POSITIVE OBLIGATION TO PRESERVE LIFE

However, Article 2(1) goes further than that. If we know that we can use a technique that is very likely to reduce the risk of death, then we should absolutely do that. That must also be a primary and paramount consideration when considering the 'best interest of the child criteria'.

If we now, also consider that some of the most common risk factors associated with people dying from restraint related positional asphyxia are; restraint going on for an extended period of time, the use of prone restraint, basket-holds, neck locks, double-seated embrace techniques, etc., then it must be consistent with Article 2(1) of the Human Rights Act and also consistent with the 'best interest of the child' criteria to eliminate such known risk factors from occurring by not using these types of techniques. This is where the use of a more restrictive technique, even a pain compliance technique is contextually imperative and possibly even crucial in the strategic risk management of physical intervention in preventing restraint related deaths. Failure to understand this puts lives at risk.

THE BEST INTEREST OF STAFF DILEMMA

A fact and basic reality is that many staff do their jobs under a cloud of fear and anxiety. They fear prosecution or are afraid of being disciplined should a child in their care get injured during a restraint. Many fear these consequences to the extent that the 'best interest of the child' criteria becomes second to their own 'best interest' criteria in not wanting to be investigated, disciplined or prosecuted.

ACTING AS A 'GOOD PARENT' SHOULD - PARENTAL RESPONSIBILITY

Under the Children Act 1989 Section 3, the meaning of 'Parental Responsibility', it states that:

> *"A person who does not have parental responsibility for a particular child; but has care of the child, may do what is reasonable in all of the circumstances of the case for the purpose of safeguarding or promoting a child's welfare".*

Therefore, in the best interests of the child criteria, anyone with parental responsibility for the safety and welfare of children must take all reasonable steps to ensure that children in their care are protected from any foreseeable and unnecessary harm (that is also good risk management practice as required under Health and Safety legislation). And, if that means using pain-compliance techniques to prevent a greater harm to the child, then that must override any self-serving or conflicting interest on behalf of the adults or agency management (school, care home, etc.,) who care for the child.

WHAT ABOUT OTHER SERVICE USERS - VULNERABLE ADULTS AND THE ELDERLY?

In this chapter we have focused primarily on the issue of pain-compliance techniques within the framework of children's legislation, primarily because there is so much documentation that relates to children, in this particular field. However, apply the same thinking and the same issues apply to staff that work with vulnerable adults and the elderly. Ultimately, they are vulnerable human beings too, aren't they?

Going back to where we started on this issue, there are many agencies who, in spite of all of the evidence, still provide instruction and guidance on the use of physical intervention, that actively state that the use of any physical intervention technique that causes intentional pain, especially if used on a vulnerable person, amounts to abuse or torture and as such must never be used within a physical intervention programme as, in their opinion, it is not in the best interest of the service user.

Once again, their opinion may be well intentioned and commendable but sadly, paradoxical. In short, omitting such techniques that could prevent a greater harm occurring is in itself an act of negligence by omission. If another child or vulnerable adult should die as a result of such omission, then there could be consequences under various legislation, including prosecution under the Corporate Manslaughter and Corporate Homicide Act 2007.

As I have already mentioned, even considering training in physical intervention is a daunting task for those of you who wish to either become trainers or who wish to commission training.

However, you must be aware of one very important fact. Whatever you decide to do, you are likely to be the one held responsible and accountable, irrespective of what others may tell you.

As such, I urge you to do your own due diligence and research this matter properly so that you are well armed to justify any decision that you make, that you could be held accountable for.

CHAPTER 5
PRONE RESTRAINT

Prone restraint is another issue that causes a lot of debate in the physical intervention world. Although a very effective method of controlling someone – because it is really hard to fight when placed on your front on the floor – the position itself also carries an increased level of risk, evidenced by the number of restraint related deaths that have been associated with the use of the position. As a result, many people are currently lobbying for a ban on the use of the prone position, especially following a number of high profile cases that have been in the press in recent years, and this is not just happening in the UK.

In the United States of America a number of US States are starting to ban the use of prone restraints following a number of deaths.

For example, the Colorado Department of Human Services in Denver is planning to ban prone restraints statewide following the death of a patient, Troy Geske, who died in August 2010 after being held in a prone restraint at the facility. Human Services director Reggie Bicha says he believes the administrative ban will save lives. Bicha says the Department plans to extend the rule to all public and private facilities that serve youths and adults, including contractors.

However, Denver is not the only US State taking such action. On the 26th August 2008 it was reported in the US press that Pennsylvania became the fifth US State to ban youth residential programs from using prone restraints, which they recognise can lead to accidental asphyxiation or sudden cardiac death. The ban in Pennsylvania - which affects all licensed Child Residential and Day Treatment Centres,

State Youth Development Centres and Youth Forestry Camps - was announced on the 14th August 2008 by the State Department of Public Welfare and came into effect on the 14th February 2009, according to department spokeswoman Stacey Witalec.

BUT WHAT ABOUT OVER HERE IN THE UK?

Well, the issue of prone restraint has been one that has been raised for many years. Yet, still today, many agencies use the prone position as a primary method of intervention, and worse still, many seem oblivious to the guidance in this area, some of which goes back many years.

For example, in 2000 a Draft Local Authority Circular was distributed as: 'Guidance' on the use of Physical Interventions for staff working with Children and Adults with Learning Disabilities and / or Autism. It stated:

> *"Policies should clearly describe unacceptable practices that might expose service users or staff to foreseeable risk of injury or psychological distress. This will include the avoidance of methods of intervention which: restrict breathing, or impact upon the person's airways, for example, holding a person in the prone position or using 'basket holds' where the person's arms are held tight across their chest by the person standing behind them."*

In 2002 the Police Complaints Authority (the forerunner to the Independent Police Complaints Commission), produced a document entitled 'Policing Acute Behavioural Disturbance - Revised Edition, March 2002', which stated that:

> *"The prone position should be avoided if at all possible, and the period that someone is restrained in the prone position needs to be minimised".*

THE HUMAN RIGHTS ACT - POSITIVE AND NEGATIVE OBLIGATIONS

As you are now aware, Article 2(1) of the Human Rights Act 1998 requires that all public authorities (including certain private companies) must promote the right to live. This means that they must take positive steps and take specific preventative or protective actions to secure an individual's right to life, especially and specifically where a known risk to life is evidenced.

Article 2 of the Human Rights Act is such a fundamentally important issue that reference was made to it in a House of Lords, and House of Commons Joint Committee on Human Rights Report on Deaths in Custody that was published in 2004.

In the section on Restraint in the Prone Position it stated the following:

> "246. Restraint in the prone position has been particularly controversial because of the dangers it carries to the patient, and it has been implicated in a number of deaths."

> "248. Reliance on prone restraint is a matter of concern for compliance with Article 2, given the known dangers of this position, evidenced by previous deaths."

> "248. ...we emphasise that Article 2 requires that patients and detainees should not be placed at risk by use of this position unless absolutely necessary to avert a greater risk to themselves or others, and that they should be restrained in this position for the shortest possible time necessary. In our view use of the prone position, and in particular prolonged use, needs to be very closely justified against the circumstances of the case, and this should be reflected in guidance. Equally importantly, those restraining a detainee should be capable of minimising the risks to him or her, through techniques to ensure, amongst other things, that airways are not blocked. They should be appropriately trained to do so."

MICHAEL MANSFIELD QC - AN OPINION OF ONE OF THE UK'S LEADING BARRISTERS

In addition to prone restraints, there are also other restraints that can increase the risk of death and one of those is a neck restraint.

For those of you who don't know him, Michael Mansfield QC is one of the UK's leading Barristers. Michael has made his name fighting cases no one else would touch. He is famous for representing clients such as; those wrongly convicted for the Guildford bombing; the family of Stephen Lawrence (the black teenager stabbed and killed by racist thugs); Jean Charles De Menezes (the Brazilian man shot at Stockwell tube station); Sally Clarke who was falsely accused and wrongfully convicted and imprisoned for more than 3 years for the murder of her two sons and the public enquiry into Bloody Sunday where 13 people died after British paratroopers opened fire during a civil rights march in Derry on 30 January 1972.

Michael Mansfield is an outspoken and highly intelligent man whom I had the pleasure and honour of interviewing recently. During the interview I asked Michael about the implications of Article 2 when considering certain physical intervention techniques and the following is what he said on the subject:

> "Time and time again Coroners have recommended that neck locks should not be used. Prone restraints should not be used".

He also goes on to state that if such knowingly dangerous techniques, that carry an evidenced risk of death, are actively used and someone dies as a result then it would be a violation of Article 2 of the Human Rights Act. In addition he also says:

> "If in fact, an authority is knowingly running the risk of saying well you can in some circumstances use something which in itself has a huge risk of death then I think they are highly culpable. I think if you have any technique which runs a risk of killing, then that method has to be outlawed".

In the UK, we are all bound by the Human Rights Act, and under Section 6 of the Act it states that it is unlawful for any public authority (and private company acting with such authority) to act in a way, which is incompatible with the new rights.

With regard to the use of physical restraint therefore, this means that state authorities and other private companies acting as public companies (quasi-public authorities), must act consistently in the first instance in proactively promoting that positive obligation. This means identifying what physical intervention techniques are likely to increase the risk of death and then finding safer alternatives that do not breach the positive obligation to preserve life as required by Article 2(1).

This is also consistent with the new amendment to the Corporate Manslaughter and Corporate Homicide Act 2007, which came into effect on the 13 September 2011. This Act makes it easier for public authorities and private organisations to be prosecuted under the Act, where a death occurs due to someone having been restrained using an authorised and badly taught body hold.

In spite of all of this many agencies today are still using the prone position as a primary method of intervention, for example, when administering a sedative injection into the buttocks of a patient. The argument generally put forward for the use of the prone position in these circumstances is that the prone position is the only position that works and is the one 'approved' for use in the organisation. In addition, some agencies have stated that if they used another position it would invalidate the license to use the drug being administered.

Yet when we explore these two main points, what we find is that agencies have never actually considered an alternative to the prone position and that the use of the position is more down to hereditary custom and practice than any actual objective assessment. In addition, one exceptional physical intervention trainer who works for a large NHS trust has been doing research into the prone position and he cannot find anything anywhere, from a medical or clinical perspective, that advocates why the prone position should be used. Furthermore, he has also been in touch with the drug companies regarding the license in relation to how these sedative drugs should be administered, and (as you have probably guessed) the license does not dictate that the drug has to be administered in the buttocks. In fact, there are in some cases, eleven other sites around the body where the drug can be administered.

My point is this. If and when a death occurs, how are you going to be able to demonstrate to a court that you have taken positive steps, consistent with Article 2 of the Human Rights Act, to evidence that you have explored alternatives to the use of the prone position and therefore that the use of the position was, by default, 'absolutely necessary' under Human Rights legislation? How are you going to prove that the 'badly taught body hold' (as described in relation to the new amendment to the Corporate Manslaughter & Corporate Homicide Act 2007) was 'authorised' for use as part of your physical intervention programme or for the administration of a sedative injection under restraint?

Interestingly BILD who will not approve any organisation that uses any form of pain-compliance technique will approve your programme if it uses prone. Therefore, if you think that you are protected because your physical intervention programme has been approved or accredited by an independent source, then the next chapter is something you should read.

OTHER TECHNIQUES THAT ALSO INCREASE RISK

Research concluded by Coventry University and published in July 2011 has shown that restraining someone who is leaning forward in a seated position for a prolonged period does increase the risk of harm or death, according to research funded by the Youth Justice Board.

Academic researchers found that those who took part in their experiments with seated restraint techniques repeatedly reported that they couldn't breathe. One volunteer was in such distress that they felt obliged to abort the experiment.

"This is the first time that this has occurred during our work on restraint," said Dr. John Parkes of Coventry University's faculty of health.

He said the experience of being unable to breathe, may cause the restrained person to panic and attempt to break out of the restraint. This in turn leads to the person restraining, applying even greater force and thereby increasing the danger.

The findings may have a bearing on cases such as that of Jimmy Mubenga, a 46-year-old Angolan, who died while being deported from Britain in 2010.

Parkes said that most of the research so far into the use of physical intervention techniques in prisons or mental health services had focused on people who were being held prone on the floor or even hogtied (when limbs are tied together). However, it is clear that deaths have occurred in other positions. This study was carried out with the intention of applying previously used methodology to seated restraint positions, including examination of the effects of body size and leaning forward during seated restraint.

Helen Shaw, co-director of Inquest, which advises the families of those who die in custody, said the research findings were significant. She said:

"We have seen at inquests, cases of people who have been struggling for their lives because they couldn't

breathe while they were being restrained. This has been misinterpreted by restraining staff to mean they were attempting to escape and they have then held them down more forcefully. However this research confirms that is not the case."

The Chief Executive of the Youth Justice Board, John Drew, said the report had been shared with relevant government departments who had been asked to *"consider the findings and take any appropriate actions to ensure that existing and future systems of restraint are adjusted accordingly".*

In a recently published Government advice document (Ref. No. DFE-00060-2011) entitled *"Use of Reasonable Force - Advice for Head Teachers, Staff and Governing Bodies"*, published in July 2011, certain physical intervention techniques were identified that presented an "unacceptable risk" when used on children and young people.

The techniques in question are:

- The 'seated double embrace' which involves two members of staff forcing a person into a sitting position and leaning them forward, while a third monitors breathing;

- The 'double basket-hold' which involves holding a person's arms across their chest; and

- The 'nose distraction technique' which involves a sharp upward jab under the nose.

Yet still today these techniques are being taught and we regularly meet members of staff who are still being taught single and double basket-holds as part of their organisation's physical intervention training programme.

CHAPTER SIX
BILD ACCREDITATION

At NFPS Ltd, we regularly get individuals and organisations contacting us to inquire about physical intervention training. One of the questions we are asked is whether or not we are BILD accredited, to which the answer is no. When we ask them why they ask, one of the most common answers we get is that they believe they are only allowed to use BILD accredited trainers and training providers because BILD accreditation is some kind of 'Nationally Recognised Standard' supported by various Government departments, that all training providers should possess and that all commissioner's of training should adhere to.

This is not to say that BILD do not do a good job. On the contrary, BILD do excellent work in the field of learning disabilities, but there seems to be a myth perpetuating throughout the physical intervention world that BILD has somehow attained 'Nationally Recognised Accreditation' status, which is also supported and promoted by various Government Departments, namely the Department of Health, the Department for Education and Skills and the Care Quality Commission.

The reality however is that BILD accreditation is only recognised by BILD itself. It is not a standard that is supported, regulated, endorsed or promoted by the Department of Health, the Department for Education and Skills, the Care Quality Commission, or Skills for Care, or indeed any other Government Department. It is merely a system of accreditation by association.

The problem arises when BILD's name appears in various Government Departmental documents, such as the 2002 Department of

Health guidance document; 'Guidance for restrictive physical interventions: How to provide safe services for people with learning disabilities and autistic spectrum disorder'. Due to this some people, including NVQ assessors and CQC Inspectors, automatically promote BILD as the only recognised accredited source. However, this is in itself misleading.

I have recently taken this matter up with the Care Quality Commission and the Department of Health who have stated that where BILD is mentioned in their documentation, it is not intended to promote BILD, because the Care Quality Commission do not promote any training provider at all.

In an e-mail sent to me on Monday 10th October 2011 from the Care Quality Commission, they stated the following:

> *"We no longer advise Providers about the most appropriate training providers to use under the Health and Social Care Act, however Skills for Care are an organisation who are able to provide specific information regarding this requirement."*

I then contacted Skills for Care who are mentioned in the above and in an e-mail sent to me on the 9th November 2011 they categorically stated the following:

> *"It is considered best practice for physical intervention training to be accredited, but this is not compulsory.*
>
> *The CQC will expect workers to demonstrate that they have the right skills, knowledge and competence to carry out their duties and it is the responsibility of the Registered Manager to ensure that this is the case.*
>
> *Therefore, it is more important that the content of the course enables the workers to achieve competence, than it is for the training to be accredited."*

I replied to this by asking the following question:

> *"Thank you for your speedy reply and clarification. Just for specific clarification, can I take it as read then, that Skills for Care does not promote BILD Accredited training above any other form of training?"*

To which, my reply from Skills for Care was:

"That is correct Mark."

In addition after pursuing the matter further with the Department of Health, I then received the following e-mail on the 15th December 2011 in response to an e-mail that I sent to them on the 28th November 2011. The relevant extract from the content of the e-mail in relation to BILD is as follows:

"Dear Mr Dawes,

My colleague [name withheld] contacted me yesterday with an update regarding your enquiry and our progress with the Department of Health (DH).

Since receiving the copy of the email response from [name withheld] that you kindly forwarded to us, [name withheld] has advised me that she has taken advice from our legal team and consulted the Department of Health about the options proposed by our legal team.

As a result of this dialogue, we have taken their views into account to amend our current guidance for inspectors about the use of restraint in regulated services.

The changes include removal of the reference to BILD as an example of an accredited source for trainers in physical intervention.

kind regards,

[name withheld]
National Customer Service Centre Officer
Customer Services
National Correspondence Team
Care Quality Commission"

However, many organisations looking to promote their business or to placate the inspectorate may not understand all of this and they will mistakenly believe it is probably easier to simply adopt the BILD Code of Practice than to do their own due diligence and challenge it. The reasoning possibly behind the decision to do so was coined beautifully by Upton Sinclair who, over 100 years ago, said: *"It is hard to get a man to understand something when his salary depends on him not understanding it."*

However, there are some who do understand the implications and who do challenge BILD's position, and the following is a written synopsis from two experienced and knowledgeable trainers who recently did just that.

AN EXPERIENCED TRAINER'S PERSPECTIVE

The names of the people concerned have been withheld by request, as has the name of their organisation. The name of the person at BILD has also been withheld and will, for the sake of anonymity, be referred to as [T]. Apart from that, the following is the exact content that was sent to me.

> *"When we attended the workshop in September this year [2011], we were looking at what was needed to accredit our training as it was identified that this 'stamp of recognition' was being asked for when advertising our training courses.*
>
> *Not long after arriving, [T] (who was delivering the workshop) was asking delegates what we already knew about BILD.*
>
> *After a couple of minutes, [T] stated that BILD would not accredit any organisation that had any material mentioning, or any practical training, that used any pain compliance techniques. [T] said that any organisation that used these methods would be unsuccessful in their application.*
>
> *When asked further about this, [T] said that she did not agree with the use of pain compliance, as it was not ethical.*
>
> *This raised a few eyebrows to say the least as there were other organisations present that deliver training in Physical Interventions & Breakaway/ Self Defence techniques.*
>
> *My colleague and I stated that we had these materials and taught the techniques in our delivery as a protection for both staff & service users, and this may include*

the use of a wristlock, etc. These would only be used as a very last resort and/or in exceptional circumstances to prevent what could be a life-threatening situation, and that if we failed to make our staff aware of this we could be legally liable.

The only answer that we got at this point from [T] was that: "there are other methods that can be used". However, we were not given any information as to what these methods were.

When pressed further [T] said that previously BILD had accepted that 'pain compliance' might be used in exceptional circumstances and this had been built into the 'Code of Practice'. However this had now been changed and had been taken out of the 2010 Code of Practice.

A little bit later, [T] told the group that it was not true that BILD would not accredit the use of 'prone restraint'. [T] said that there are organisations accredited by BILD who teach and use prone restraint techniques, as long as there was a thorough risk assessment, (remember BILD state that they accredit organisations that support children & adults with a learning disability, children & adults with Autistic spectrum conditions, pupils with special educational needs, children with social & emotional difficulties associated with behaviours that challenge etc.!!).

Obviously at this point my colleague and I plus quite a few of the rest of the group were getting very confused about these statements.

My colleague pointed out the very real risks regarding the use of prone and the dangers of positional asphyxia (Zoe Fairley, Anthony Pinder, etc.) and therefore how could BILD accredit organisations advocating these techniques, as opposed to the use of pain compliance techniques that would possibly prevent someone from being seriously injured or possibly killed?

[T] replied: "I didn't say that I agreed with the use of prone, but it fits in with our standards for Accreditation", but by this time [T] was pretty defensive!

Really the rest of the day was downhill from there on!

This clearly went against the Principles & Legislation that we had been taught regarding 'Reasonable Force' and we were very concerned as to whether we should be continuing with the BILD accreditation process.

I think we had about lost the will to live by this point!"

ETHICAL AND MORAL TRAINING PROVISION

At this stage, I want to pick up on one point in the above extract, in particular the view of [T] who did not agree with the use of pain compliance, as it was not 'ethical'. I hear people bang on about ethics all of the time so I thought I'd just nip this in the bud here and now and clearly define what it actually means.

There are many schools of ethics in Western philosophy, which can be roughly divided into three main areas. The first, drawing on the work of Aristotle, holds that virtues (such as justice, charity, and generosity) are qualities that motivate us to act in ways that benefit both the person possessing them and that person's society as a whole.

The second approach makes the concept of duty central to morality. This basically means making the conscious decision between doing what is right as opposed to doing what we know to be wrong.

The third is utilitarianism, which promotes that the guiding principle of conduct should be of the greatest happiness or benefit of the greatest number of people

In addition to ethics, morals are also concerned with the principles of right and wrong behaviour and the goodness or badness of human character.

Being 'moral' or having a 'morality' has been defined as being concerned with or adhering to a particular code of interpersonal behaviour that is considered right or acceptable in a particular society. To act with morality therefore, means we adopt and promote high principles of proper conduct.

In short, someone who is considered to be a moral person believes that they have a duty to, and a benefit in demonstrating good behaviour consistently for the benefit of their fellow citizens or their society as a whole.

They have a utilitarian perspective on their purpose in life, which means that what they do is designed to be useful and practical rather than just attractive, and that benefit must be obtained for the greater good of the majority in a particular society with the primary aim of improving the quality of life for everyone.

My argument therefore, is that if we are acting with good intention and consciously making a decision to do what is right for the right reasons, we are being ethical.

Also, if we are demonstrating high principles of proper conduct for the benefit of others in our society and are doing something that is designed to be practical with the primary aim of improving the quality of life – or indeed promoting the positive obligation to preserve life, then we must be acting morally.

Maybe it's just me, but how can a BILD representative openly state that they disagree with a technique that could save a life on the basis of it being unethical?

Furthermore, statements such as this by someone with influence over others can create systematic failings in a physical intervention system if they are adopted and implemented without proper forethought. In health and safety terms giving such advice and producing such guidance are classified as 'knowledge-based' and 'rule-based' mistakes as defined by HSG48, which you will learn more about later on in this book.

THE POTENTIAL DRAWBACKS AND LIABILITIES

The drawback for commissioning agencies (local authorities, care homes, schools, etc.,) is that they may decide to engage the services of BILD accredited trainers, primarily on the basis that they believe they are accredited to a nationally recognised and competent standard and are supported and promoted by various Government Departments.

However this is not the case. You will simply be engaging the services of an organisation, which is recognised by BILD and no one else.

And if you are a training provider you should also be aware of the fact that BILD accreditation is not a shield against protection from prosecution.

In BILD's own code of practice it states that training providers should balance the needs of service users: *"with the rights of staff members /employees and obligations of employers under relevant legislation and guidance[1]"*. Yet, as we have already seen in the section on pain compliance and prone restraint, BILD's view is different from ours and I will leave it up to you, the reader, to decide which one you prefer.

I believe that the misconception about BILD accreditation can and does leave many commissioning agencies vulnerable and very culpable.

As many of you reading this will already know, we (NFPS Ltd.) are not BILD accredited, nor are we likely to become so, as we know that BILD accreditation is not a Nationally Recognised Accreditation scheme or standard.

We have spent an awful lot of time and effort in attempting to get to the bottom of what BILD accreditation actually means, who supports it, and whether or not it is a recognised form of accreditation and below is a series of e-mail exchanges between ourselves and various Government Agencies, some of whom, such as CSCI (the Commission for Social Care Inspection) were the forerunner of the Care Quality Commission (CQC) and Ofsted.

WHAT IS BILD ACCREDITATION?

BILD's Behavioural Support Development Manager contacted us on the 12th June 2007 in response to an article we published on our web site. His email stated:

> *"We do not train you, we assess your ability to deliver training to other organisations within a framework of recognised best practice. If accredited, you will be able to use your status as an accredited training organisation as a marketing tool. BILD do not teach physical intervention skills. BILD manages an accreditation scheme for training organisations that do teach such skills. BILD does provide training around the issues of behaviour support and the use of PI."*

---

1   BILD Code of Practice for the use and reduction of restrictive physical interventions – Third Edition – August 2010

In short, BILD do not teach physical intervention but assess your ability to deliver physical intervention training. Isn't that the same as being assessed by a driving examiner who hasn't passed their driving test?

IS BILD ACCREDITATION A NATIONALLY RECOGNISED QUALIFICATION OR SCHEME FOR PHYSICAL INTERVENTION TRAINERS?

BILD's opinion in 2006:

> *"At present the BILD Scheme is the only national accreditation scheme for trainers in physical intervention. The BILD scheme is supported by the DoH / DfES through the joint guidance on the use of PI in services for children/adults with Learning Disability / Autistic Spectrum Disorder and Pupils with Special Educational needs. I have attached a copy of the guidance for your information. As stated above, the DoH /DfES sponsored the development of the scheme and maintain an active interest in it.*
>
> *In addition, CSCI have included in their guidance to inspectors, around the use of PI, comments on accredited status of training provided to care services."*

Department for Education and Skills response:
dated 29 November 2006:

> *"You state that BILD are promoting their Nationally Recognised status on the basis that it is approved and accredited by the DfES. I am able to confirm, once again, that DfES are unable to approve or accredit any provider in this field, and that it is for the commissioners themselves to determine the appropriateness of the training against local need.*
>
> *I can also confirm that DfES officials do not sit on BILD's accreditation panel."*

My e-mail to CSCI dated 20th October 2006

"Dear Sir / Madam

Re: Commission for Social Care Inspection - Guidance Log for Children's Homes

"I would very much appreciate it if you would you please clarify for me whether CSCI Inspectors are expected to advise on what method / system of physical intervention should be used within the scope of the child care organisations that CSCI Inspectors visit.

In the Guidance supporting NMS 22.8 it states in paragraph 2 that:

"The expectation from the DfES/DH guidance regarding interventions with children (or adults) who have learning disabilities and/or autistic spectrum disorders is that training should normally be 'provided by trainers who are accredited under the BILD Code of Practice on Training Staff in the use of Physical Interventions' (section 14, Implementation, 14.1)."

The inference drawn from item 22.8 is that CSCI is supporting and thus 'advising' that training should normally be provided by only trainers accredited under the BILD Code of Practice."

CSCI's reply on behalf of Department of Health:
1 November 2006:

*"The CSCI does not support specific trainers. BILD trainers are not universally endorsed by this statement. In short, whether or not staff have been trained in a particular method of restraint by an accredited training agency **is not the most important factor**; [their use of bold type, not mine] individual cases should be assessed on the basis of actual practice of restraint in the home and whether this practice meets the Regulations and Standards."*

DOES THE DFES / DOH RECOMMEND ANY PREFERRED RESTRAINT METHOD OVER ANY OTHER?

Reply received from DfES dated 17/03/04.

*"We in DfES do not promote particular providers or dis-
courage the use of others. The decision is one that has
to be taken locally."*

DOES THE NATIONAL CARE STANDARDS COMMISSION (NOW CSCI) RECOMMEND ANY PREFERRED RESTRAINT METHOD OVER ANY OTHER?

Reply to us from National Care Standards Commission, Children's
Rights Directorate dated 12/08/03.

*"As a general response to this enquiry, it should be clear-
ly understood that the official policy of this Commission
is that it does not, and will not, provide specific advice or
recommendations, or express any preference, as to any
particular method of physical restraint, over and above
any other. It is for the provider to identify techniques
which are intended to keep Children safe and compliant
with the requirements of standards; and it is for NCSC
inspectors to judge the application of these on their individual merits."*

By now I think that you are getting the picture. For over eight years
we have undertaken our own research into BILD's physical intervention accreditation scheme, and what we have found is that it is an
area full of myths and misconceptions and smoke and mirrors.

WHAT ABOUT AN INSPECTORS COMPETENCE IN RELATION TO PHYSICAL INTERVENTION?

Another area, in which we supported our clients, was when an inspector arrived at a home to undertake an inspection and make
remarks or recommendations to the home management about the
use of physical intervention. This worried some of our care home
clients as they felt that if they implemented the inspector's recommendations they would be actually increasing the risk to their
service users and staff.

However, they also felt under pressure to implement the recommendations, because they knew that the inspector had the power
to impose sanctions if they didn't, which could result in a home
being downgraded and the organisation losing placements and
future business.

As a result, we wanted to ascertain what level of professional competency an inspector would have to allow them to make recommendations on physical intervention, so I sent the following e-mail to CSCI:

E-mail to CSCI, 12th September 2005
Re: Inspectors Competence in relation to Physical Restraint

> *"Could you please inform me what specific competencies a CSCI inspector will have in relation to their ability to make comments such as those above? In short, what training do they have in physical restraint and what competencies / qualifications do they have in this area? I ask this as many of the comments I am coming across seem very subjective and not based on any correct legal interpretation."*

Reply from CSCI on 13th September 2005:

> *"Starting with your final question, inspectors observations about the use of restraint will be based on the regulations and standards and other relevant documents such as the United Nations Convention on the Rights of the Child. Whether or not, inspectors have received training in the use of physical restraint, will depend very much on their own past experience and training. Such training is not part of the required training for inspectors."*

Clearly CSCI was not providing training for their inspectors, hence why they themselves should not be making any recommendations on the use of physical intervention.

As a result of undertaking our own due-diligence in this area we could therefore see no benefit in becoming 'BILD accredited' as the accreditation is only really accreditation by a private company and nothing more. That is why we are not BILD accredited.

CHAPTER SEVEN
PHYSICAL INTERVENTION AND THE SECURITY INDUSTRY AUTHORITY

As from August 2011 all trainers providing physical intervention training for Door Supervisors are required to hold a Level 3 Award for Deliverers of Physical Intervention Training in the Private Security Industry (QcF). This Level 3 Award allows trainers to teach the Level 2 Physical Intervention Module (Unit 4) of the Door Supervisors License to Practice Award so that door supervisors can obtain their SIA License, which allows them to work on a door.

The scope of the qualification however, is that it only allows door supervisors to be taught how to use: *"non-aggressive physical skills to protect self and others from assault", and "low-level restrictive and non-restrictive holding and escorting techniques"*.

The use of higher-level defensive techniques (which may involve striking or kicking), or more restrictive physical intervention techniques (which may involve the use of pain-compliance techniques) however, fall outside the scope of this award and are not to be taught as part of the door supervisors license to practice award.

This has had a mixed response from the door supervision community, some of whom are of the opinion that the scope of the training doesn't go far enough in providing door supervisors with physical intervention skills that meet the reality of the levels of violence they are expected to control.

Others however, see it as a step in the right direction and a move away from the old 'bouncer' image of door supervisors to a more professional branding of the industry.

However, what must be understood is that the scope of training provided, consistent with the SIA's requirements, is the minimum necessary for licensing purposes only, and if any other training is required to meet the level of risk that door supervisors face, then this must be given consistent with the findings of any assessment of risk, as required under the duty of care owed to staff and others in line with current Health and Safety legislation.

Also, the scope of the SIA training doesn't restrict the individual's right to use force consistent with UK statute and common law that applies to any private citizen, and these points have been clarified by the SIA in an e-mail to me which reads as follows:

> *"As a general comment, the purpose of the SIA training is to establish the standard required for someone to qualify for a licence. We don't restrict training; we encourage employers and individuals to get any further appropriate training where it is necessary for their specific needs.*
>
> *In terms of the training itself, this includes both knowledge and skills. The knowledge deals with a wider scope of activities, and includes knowledge of the medical/legal risks, etc., involved in any physical intervention. The skills are the 'low level restrictive or non-restrictive'. The definition of non-restrictive, the awarding body guidance gives, is the one where the subject can walk away, however the definition of low-level restrictive means that they could be applied against someone's will, if for example they were escorting someone from a premises that they did not want to leave.*
>
> *As we discussed, the definition of low-level restrictive excludes (via the programme approval criteria) wrist/arm locks, strikes, and any techniques that involve the neck, etc. That would fall into the definition of highly restrictive intervention and we advise people to take this sort of training where necessary.*
>
> *In terms of the legislation, we say that the licence-linked qualification in no way changes the obligation of an in-*

dividual to act in accordance with the law on the use of force that applies to any private citizen, and that the training does not change the employer's legal obligations with regard to ensuring the safety and security of customers and employees. We make it clear that this includes the need for any additional training that a Door Supervisor may require that is identified via an employer's risk assessment of a particular venue or event.

We do not mention Human Rights Legislation by name, but make it clear that individuals must comply with the law."

What this means is that where necessary, employers may need to provide additional training if they feel that the scope of what the SIA provides does not provide their staff with the ability to safely and competently control the level of violence and aggression that they are exposed to whilst at work.

But obviously, additional training means additional costs, and who should pay? Should it be the door supervisor; the agency that he or she works for, the landlord of the pub or the nightclub owner who employs them on a sub-contracted basis? Well that's a discussion that will fall outside the scope of this book. However, where it is apparent that additional training is needed - it should be given. That is a legal requirement.

However, whilst the debate goes on about who should pay for any additional training, we are highly likely to have door supervisors working on the doors of pubs, clubs and nightclubs who have only received the basic, low level training, designed as a minimum standard for the purposes of licensing only. They will also most likely be working with people who obtained their license prior to the need to undertake any physical intervention training and who are, by default, untrained.

So what happens when a door supervisor, trained to a bare minimum standard in *"low-level restrictive and non-restrictive holding and escorting techniques"*, has to deal with an extremely violent and aggressive individual whose physically violent behaviour falls outside of the scope of bare minimum training that they have received as part of the door supervisors licensing training?

What happens when the skills that they have been taught don't work or fail? And what do they do when possibly letting someone go is not an option due to the risk posed to themselves or others?

Well the answer is simple - they revert to type. They revert to what they probably would have done prior to the training taking place, such as using neck-locks and the prone position; positions, which we know, should not be used due to the high level of risk associated with them. In short we end up with a situation whereby the training designed or implemented to reduce risk actually ends up increasing it. And this doesn't just happen to door supervisors, it happens to people who work in the Care industries too.

CHAPTER EIGHT
THE 'RODNEY-KING' EFFECT

I recently received a report about a restraint incident where a member of staff during the restraint, hit the person being restrained and told them to "shut the **** up". This was because the person being restrained bit into the member of staff's arm. Prior to this incident, the member of staff was suspended from work whilst an investigation took place under child protection procedures.

I can also recall a dynamic pressurised training scenario a while ago where two very large male police officers were attempting to physically control a smaller and slightly built female instructor. During the scenario the female instructor said; "you're hurting me" to which one of the men, replied; "if you don't stop struggling I'll break your ******* arm".

From one perspective it would seem that such behaviour is unacceptable, especially from staff expected to be 'professional' and 'caring' in their approach to dealing with situations of high arousal, and particularly if the staff had been given training as to how they should react and how they should behave.

So why would this occur? Why would staff hit and swear at a restrained person and why would two large, and supposedly well-trained police officers, threaten to break a small female's arm?

The answer would seem to lie in what I now refer to as the 'Rodney King' effect.

In recent years many police departments in the US have banned high-speed chases. This is because about 300 people are killed every year in the US during such chases, and it isn't just because of what happens during the chase, it is also because of what happens after the chase.

During a high-speed chase, police officers become highly aroused, because pursuing a subject at high speed is going to trigger the primitive fight and flight response. In this state, police officers enter the dangerous area of 'high arousal' and what they do next can have massive implications.

An example of this was the Los Angeles riot, which was started because of what LA police officers did to Rodney King at the end of a high-speed chase. In short, they beat him to death, and this phenomenon was repeated again in Miami in 1986.

According to Malcolm Gladwell in his book 'Blink', three of the major race riots in the US over the past 25 years were caused by what police officers did at the end of a high-speed chase.

During these chases, officers reported 'high levels of adrenaline' – like a runners high, with increased feelings of 'euphoria'. They reported losing perspective, in short, their vision became tunnelled; they lost depth perception and also became shortsighted. Their hearing also shut down, and this is not unusual. In research undertaken by Professor Dave Grossman in relation to Combat Psychology, we lose somewhere in the region of 80% of our ability to hear when our heart rate increases in these kinds of incidents. In essence the officers in these chases get 'wrapped up in the chase', which was best described by Malcom Gladwell in his book when he stated – "a dog in the hunt doesn't stop to scratch its fleas".

In many of these situations officers can't even speak normally – they shout, and immediately after the event many can't even use a radio because they are shaking so much.

One high-ranking Los Angeles police officer, Bob Martin, said that in the Rodney King case, King's beating was 'precisely what one would expect' when two parties – both with soaring heartbeats and predatory cardiovascular reactions – encounter each other after a chase. At one key point during the Rodney King arrest, one of the senior officers at the scene told the officers to "back off", but they ignored his instruction. Why? Because - they simply didn't hear him.

In the situation in the first paragraph, where a member of staff hit and swore at the person being restrained, the actual restraint had been going on for around four hours! It had been a violent restraint during which a violent and prolonged struggle had taken place. During the struggle the staff involved had been assaulted many times. They had had their faces gouged, hair pulled, bitten, kicked, punched and spat at. They were also under other forms of pressure too. The system of restraint, that the staff at this organisation, were trained in, absolutely prohibited the use of any restrictive technique – especially and explicitly any technique that may inadvertently or intentionally cause discomfort or pain - because the person being restrained, a 14 year-old child in this case, is deemed to be a 'vulnerable person'.

The member of staff who struck the child was immediately placed under investigation due to child protection procedures for striking and swearing at the child. He was suspended from work for three months while the investigation took place.

In the end, the member of staff was found to have used reasonable force in the situation, but he was still given a written warning for swearing at the child, which stayed on his record.

My point is this. If staff are being trained in systems of intervention that do not work and are therefore ineffective at controlling the person being restrained, the 'Rodney King' effect will be an effect waiting for a cause.

If inspectors from the various inspectorates continue to give subjective and adverse advice on physical intervention – advice that should not be given by persons not competently trained in the psychology and practice of the skill they are commenting on - that 'bullies' organisations into adopting inappropriate and ineffective systems of restraint, the 'Rodney King' effect will be waiting in the wings in anticipation of a curtain call.

If training providers and Government appointed Regulatory Bodies do not listen to those who need the training, and continue to provide weak systems of work that are designed to be nice by being politically correct, then the 'Rodney King' effect, like Frankenstein's monster, will be brought to life again and again.

As a society we cannot give those staff empowered to protect and care for others, or to enforce the law, inadequate and incorrect advice, insufficient and weak guidance and poor training based on flawed and outdated methods of instruction and then, when the system fails them, blame them and hang them out to dry for failing to make an unsafe system work.

CHAPTER NINE
THE RISE OF POLITICAL EXPEDIENCY AND THE FALL OF CREDIBLE TRAINING

Just over a year ago, I was having dinner with a very close friend and professional colleague of mine called Peter Boatman. Peter, for those of you who don't know him, was one of the UK's leading experts on the use of physical force. Peter told me was that he was consistently coming across organisations whose policies are flawed to the point of being basically illegal. What he meant was that these policies don't just limit what someone can do and dictate physical interventions that are unsuitable and insufficient, they go even further than that by actually stripping an employed individual of their legal rights.

He was telling me that some of the policies that he had reviewed during his work as an expert witness included phrases such as:

> *"In the event that a staff member is attacked by a client, they may use breakaway skills, but may not use self defence methods".*

> *"Notwithstanding the risk to staff, the use of strikes is expressly prohibited and the use of any form of pain compliance technique during a physical intervention is also prohibited"*

Peter's view was that bad policy is brought about by a combination of factors including:

1. Incorrect advice from managers and executives who do not understand the law regarding self-protection, restraint and use of force.

2. Insufficient training for managers, or in many cases a complete lack of training in matters relating to use of force and physical interventions.

3. Managers attempting to limit litigation by watering down advice and guidance to staff, which places an unrealistic and unreasonable limit on the member of staff's legal right to properly respond to violence and threats of violence.

4. Deliberately misleading advice and guidance given by training providers, who themselves lack the detailed knowledge necessary to properly construct and deliver realistic task-related training.

5. Lack of hard data from the operational setting; lack of a detailed reporting system and lack of overall strategy in addressing violence against staff by way of a structured use of information.

Many other eminent and professionally competent people who know what they are talking about also share the points raised by Peter. Gary Slapper, Professor of Law and Director of the Open University's Law Faculty, recently told me that: *"many companies, in aiming to reduce their liability, produce policies that actually do the opposite."*

So what is the net effect of all this 'politically expedient' advice and guidance? The bottom line is – people get hurt or even killed unnecessary.

POLITICIANS INSTEAD OF EXPERTS

Peter went on to say that:

> *"The problem as I see it, is that trainers and managers have become 'sector politicians'. Instead of becoming experts in their chosen profession, they politicise about what should be done instead of doing it. Instead of giving their staff correct and legally accurate advice they give a watered down version of it, which fits their politically motivated agenda, an agenda, that in many cases, doesn't have the member of staff's best interests at heart, but an agenda motivated by political correctness. In short, they would rather give their staff training that is 'nice' than training in what is 'necessary'. Why – because seemingly you can't get into trouble for doing something 'nice'. Really? The fact is they are wrong."*

Why would supposedly intelligent managers do this? It's possibly because this is a motivation commonly based on fear. Fear of failure and of losing their job and a fear of possibly not wanting to look stupid, by admitting that they don't know what to do. This fear then manifests itself in advice, which although may have a veneer of 'niceness' about it, is none-the less, incorrect and potentially illegal and does nothing more than place the member of staff and others at an increased risk of harm, and both the individual manager and the organisation, at greater risk of criminal and/or civil litigation.

Challenge this however, and you will face another issue. Challenge the 'corporate strategic line' formulated by these unaccountable individuals with no professional competence and you face being marginalised, targeted and even in some cases disciplined. So what should staff do? Should they act in the best interests of the service user (as required by the Children Act 1989 for example) or in their own self-interest based on a fear of being disciplined and possibly losing their job? The choice isn't hard for many of them.

However, the real problem arises when the training techniques used, do not work and when someone gets injured, or worse - killed. What happens then is an attempt to blame the individual who used the skills that were likely to fail anyway, and the individual member of staff is then confronted with statements such as:

"If you had used the technique properly - it would have worked" and *"you had the training why didn't you use what you were taught?"*

So not only has the organisational management created a system with failure built in, but when that failure manifests itself the member of staff is hung out to dry. It is similar to a mechanic not tightening the wheel nuts on a car wheel, resulting in the wheel coming off and causing a major road traffic accident and then attempting to blame the driver for not driving correctly.

To compound this, we also have trainers and training organisations who, in an attempt to increase business or win tenders, sell their soul to the devil by developing training programmes to meet the politically expedient whims of the flawed organisational strategy and in some cases, incorrect or weak and ineffective advice and guidance issued by Government Departments, as opposed to challenging that advice and offering a legally correct and workable alternative.

"Integrity without knowledge is weak and useless, and knowledge without integrity is dangerous and dreadful."

Samuel Johnson (1709 - 1784)

In the final chapter of my book *'Understanding Reasonable Force'*, I wrote the following:

"The most important aspect, that I believe a person can promote through their day-to-day activity, is integrity. Without integrity a person shows by their deeds that they do not value that which they possess or give to others. Lack of integrity identifies itself as a lack of the understanding of a person's professional subject in a holistic way by the presentation of divided interests through a person's thoughts, words and deeds. To search for integrity, allows a person to become one with themselves, and to give all of themselves for the benefit of others without conscious objection. To find integrity, one must first seek the knowledge required to underpin one's own need for answers to questions, that create a doorway for doubt to enter, or worse, the opinions of people that have no integrity."

We should all strive to conduct ourselves with integrity so that the approach to what we do is consistent and based on factual based evidence and up to date knowledge and information.

I think now, more than ever, the words of Samuel Johnson should be seriously heeded by those individuals who are privileged and empowered with having the responsibility for the health, safety and welfare of other human beings placed in their care.

As for my good friend Peter Boatman, sadly he died in October 2010. Peter was an inspiration for me, not only professionally, but also personally and he is greatly missed, but his professionalism lives on in my work and in the work of many other people who will always strive to reach the bar that Peter set so high. For me, Peter was a man who possessed the highest level of integrity and who lived his life by those values every day. We can all learn something from Pete's example.

CHAPTER TEN
PHYSICAL INTERVENTION AND HEALTH AND SAFETY

The basis of British health and safety law is the Health and Safety at Work Act 1974 This Act sets out the general duties employers have towards employees and members of the public, and which employees have to themselves and to each other.

Section 2 of the Act places an obligation on the employer to ensure the health, safety and welfare of all of their staff whilst at work. This means that employees are provided with the correct; information, instruction, training and supervision, to enable them to do what they are employed to do, to a professionally competent standard. This is a requirement under Section 2(2)(c) of the Act. This means that any member of staff expected to physical intervene must be competently trained to do so.

Section 3 of the Act states that: *"It shall be the duty of every employer to conduct his undertaking in such a way as to ensure so far as is reasonably practicable that persons not in their employment are not exposed to risks to their health and safety"*. That means that the employer has a duty of care to others not in their employment, and in physical intervention terms this means the member of the public or service user who is likely to be restrained.

As physical intervention is an activity which places staff and others (including the subject being restrained) at risk, any failure to train staff properly and provide the correct information and instruction, can lead to the organisation being held accountable and prosecuted for a breach of Sections 2 or 3 of the Act, if, for example, untrained or poorly trained staff physically intervene and someone gets hurt.

In addition, Section 7 of the Act requires that employees take reasonable care of themselves and others who may be affected by their acts (what they do) and their omissions (what they fail to do - that they should have done). In relation to physical intervention this would mean that employees have a responsibility to do what they have been trained to do and not, for example, intentionally act negligently by ignoring any safe system of work that the employer has put in place for them.

Furthermore, Section 37 of Health and Safety at Work Act 1974 allows action to be taken against individual senior managers where a failure can be attributed to their neglect, consent or connivance. The words "consent" and "connivance" imply that the senior management had knowledge and that a decision was made based on such knowledge.

In one case, the Court of Appeal considered that "consent" required that the defendant knew the material facts that constituted the offence by the body corporate and had agreed to conduct it's business on the basis of those facts, ignorance of the law being no defence.

"Neglect" however, does not necessarily require knowledge on the senior managements part of the material facts giving rise to the breach or breaches, and can include the situation where she or he ought to have been aware of those circumstances.

In simple language, this means that if the senior management of an organisation know that staff are taking risks, for example, using physical intervention techniques that should not be used or allowing staff to be put in situations where they may be expected to restrain on their own, then they can be prosecuted if and when someone gets injured or killed as a result.

THE HEALTH AND SAFETY (OFFENCES) ACT 2008

In January 2009 the new Health and Safety (Offences) Act 2008 came into force which now raises the maximum penalties available to the courts, in respect of certain health and safety offences.

As the previous law stood, individuals found to be in breach of sections 7 or 37 of the Act could face a fine not exceeding £5,000 on

summary trial, or an unlimited fine on indictment. The new Act, however, raises the maximum summary fine to £20,000 and introduces
a term of 12 months imprisonment on summary trial, whilst a term
of 2 years imprisonment and/or an unlimited fine will be available on
indictment.

The new Act also makes imprisonment available following a breach
of the general health and safety duties imposed on employers under
sections 2 and 3 of the Health and Safety at Work Act 1974, and of
particular note are the sections of Act relating to individual liability. This means that employees themselves can be prosecuted under
section 7 of Act if they have not taken reasonable care for the health
and safety of themselves or other persons affected by their acts or
omissions, or where they have not co-operated with their employers
in health and safety matters.

In addition to the powers conferred in Section 37 of the Health and
Safety at Work Act 1974, an offence will also have been committed
under the Corporate Manslaughter and Corporate Homicide Act
2007, if failings by an organisation's senior management are a substantial element in any gross breach of the duty of care owed to the
organisation's employees or members of the public, which results in
death. If found guilty the maximum penalty is an unlimited fine and
imprisonment, and the court can additionally make a publicity order
requiring the organisation to publish details of its conviction and fine.
This means that the guilty company will now have to advertise that
it has been found guilty of the crime of Corporate Manslaughter –
imagine the impact of that on a business.

UNDERTAKING RISK ASSESSMENTS

To comply with the general duty of care owed under sections 2
and 3 of the Health and Safety at Work Act 1974, employers must
ensure that a suitable and sufficient risk assessment of the activity
of physical intervention is carried out as required by Regulation 3(1)
Management of Health and Safety at Work Regulations 1999. The
aim of such risk assessments are to identify any hazards associated
with the activity of physical intervention and the potential severity
of the harm that could be caused by those hazards, and then put
control measures in place to eliminate or reduce those foreseeable
risks to the lowest possible level.

For example, an organisation may have vulnerable people in its care who self harm, and under the duty of care owed to the vulnerable person, the organisation may require staff to intervene to prevent any serious harm occurring. In risk assessing this activity the assessment may identify that staff may be exposed to the hazard of a service user self harming with a sharp blade or knife or even a shard of glass or sharp piece of metal. The potential severity of risk would be that staff could be seriously injured or killed, if they intervene. In such cases control measures would have to be implemented that reduced that risk to its lowest possible level consistent with the duty of care owed to staff, either by providing staff with appropriate personal protective equipment to reduce the risk of them being harmed, or by eliminating the need for them to physically intervene in such situations altogether.

MANUAL HANDLING

In addition to that, because physical intervention is an activity that requires staff to gain control of a subject by human effort, it must also be treated as a 'manual handling' activity. Therefore, employers and training providers must undertake, and be able to demonstrate if required, a manual handling risk assessment for the activity of physical intervention, consistent with the Manual Handling Operations Regulations 1992.

These Regulations state that employers have a duty to its staff to avoid Manual Handling activities if there is a possibility of injury. If this cannot be done then they must reduce the risk of injury as far as it is reasonably practicable. This would, for example, mean the promotion of physical intervention techniques consistent with good manual handling principles and practices such as: keeping the back straight and keeping the load (in this case the person being restrained) close to the body, and the elimination of poor manual handling techniques that involve any unnecessary twisting and turning of the back and bending over.

AGEING AND THE SKELETAL SYSTEM

Bone is a living tissue and like the rest of the body suffers from degeneration. As we age, the amount of bone mass decreases and there is a change in the make-up of the bone, resulting in the bones becoming less elastic.

Intervertebral discs also undergo change as we age. In a young person the pulpy centre contains up to 85% water, but as we get older a gradual dehydration takes place. This effectively weakens the disc and lowers the level of loading it can tolerate. In old age these changes manifest themselves in the form of height loss, hunched backs and greater susceptibility for hip fractures.

Therefore as a general rule of thumb, younger fit people will have more natural fitness and ability for manual handling and physical intervention which will degenerate with time as they get older. This is an important factor when assessing the manual handling risks associated with physical intervention and when doing so, consideration has to be given to the age of the people likely to be restrained, balanced against the ages of those attempting to engage the physical control.

For example, if two or three 45 year-old care workers are expected to physically control a fitter and more agile 15 year-old youth, we need to devise skills that reduce the risk to them and we'll cover that later on in this book.

There is now substantial international acceptance of both the scale of manual handling problems and methods of prevention. Modern medical and scientific knowledge stresses the importance of an ergonomic approach to remove or reduce the risk of manual handling injury. Ergonomics is sometimes described as 'fitting the job to the person', rather than the 'person to the job'. The ergonomic approach, therefore, looks at manual handling as a whole. It takes into account a range of relevant factors, including the nature of the task, the load, the working environment and individual capability. This approach is central to the European Directive on manual handling, and to the Regulations.

FINDING ALTERNATIVES TO PHYSICAL INTERVENTION

In terms of physical intervention, this means not only ensuring that the techniques used, match the ability of skill of the members of staff being expected to physically intervene (fitting the job to the person), but also looking at alternatives to physical intervention by human effort by the use of equipment that is fit for purpose, such as handcuffs, or emergency response belts, or even something as simple as the temporary locking of a door, and all of these options are control measures that should be identifiable in the assessment of risk.

For example, my colleague John Steadman and I were once asked if we had a technique for getting someone out of a toilet who didn't want to come out. In the first instance (under the basic concepts of reasonable force) we asked if it was really necessary to do so. If it isn't necessary, because there is no risk of harm, then a use of force option isn't an option. Secondly, if a team of staff were likely to have to remove someone forcibly from a toilet what potential hazards are they likely to encounter? Well for starters, a toilet is a confined space as defined by The Confined Spaces Regulations 1997, and under Regulation 4(1) it states that: *"No person at work shall enter a confined space to carry out work for any purpose unless it is not reasonably practicable to achieve that purpose without such entry."*

In addition, if someone has just been to the toilet and they know you are coming for them to remove them by force, they may have a 'present' for you when you burst through the door. If this 'present' is 'toxic' and / or contains germs that could spread disease, it is defined as a 'substance that is hazardous to health' under the COSHH Regulations (Control of Substances Hazardous to Health Regulations 2002) which requires organisations to assess the risk of such exposure and put the required control measures in place.

These are just some examples of how health and safety legislation should be implemented when considering the use of physical intervention in the workplace. It does not take long to get things right, it just takes a bit of effort and it is definitely worth it in the end. All of the resources you need, can be found on the Health and Safety Executives website at: www.hse.gov.uk

SINGLE PERSON RESTRAINT

One question that arises in many conversations is whether a trained member of staff can restrain another individual on their own. This question is normally driven by financial restrictions and departmental budgets, and can be compounded by a lack of any approved code of practice or regulatory guidance. The following is my professional view on the issue based on years of operational, training and coaching experience.

It is not unlawful for an individual to physically intervene on their own, because no law prohibits it. However, as physical intervention is an activity that carries with it a degree of operational risk, it must be suitably and sufficiently assessed for risk, in line with the Regulations mentioned earlier. This is a legal requirement.

In addition, the HSE has also published guidance on Lone Working, which you can review and download by going to:

www.hse.gov.uk/contact/faqs/workalone.htm

So, at this point let us summarise what we already know.

1. Physical intervention can be generally defined as: *"The positive application of force for the purpose of overcoming a subject's resistance with the intention of removing the subject's liberty."*

2. A single person at work is commonly known as a 'lone worker'.

3. Health and Safety Executive's definition of a 'lone worker' is: *"People who work by themselves without close or direct supervision"*.

4. For the purposes of this book, and taking the above definitions into account, we have further defined a 'single-person restraint' as being:

5. *"The positive application for force, by a person working on their own, or in isolation, for the purpose of overcoming a subject's resistance with the intention of removing the subject's liberty"*.

Therefore, although there is no specific legal prohibition concerning an individual intervening on their own, the Health and Safety Executive would possibly classify the action as a 'lone working activity' based on the Health and Safety Executives definition of 'lone workers'.

To summarise so far, any individual who is expected to physically control another person on their own, primarily because they are likely to be placed in situations by their employer, where they will be working by themselves, possibly without close or direct supervision and without additional staff or on-going inadequate staffing levels, is, by definition, a 'lone worker'.

WHO IS RESPONSIBLE FOR 'LONE WORKERS'?

Employers have responsibility for the health, safety and welfare at work of all of their employees, including those used on a casual, part-time and voluntary basis. This will include for example any self-employed people they may use, including sub-contractors.

Employers are also responsible for any third party that may be affected by the actions and omission of their staff, including the person being restrained and any other non-employed person who could possibly become injured as a result of staff actions or omissions such as a member of the public.

CAN THIS RESPONSIBILITY AND LIABILITY BE TRANSFERRED TO ANOTHER PERSON?

In short, the answer is No. The employer has a responsibility to extend a duty of care to all of it's employees to ensure their health, safety and welfare whilst at work, and that responsibility cannot be transferred to any other person, including those people who work alone.

What this basically means in essence is that any employer, be it a care home provider, a school, local education authority, a pub, club or nightclub, a NHS trust, a Security Company, etc., cannot and should not expect staff to physically intervene and restrain anyone on their own. If they did and an injury; or worse still a fatality, occurred to a member of staff or the person being restrained, then the employer could be held liable.

THE HUMAN RIGHTS IMPLICATIONS

As you now know, Article 2(1) of the Human Rights Act 1998 imposes a duty on all Public Authorities to take positive and pro-active steps to promote and preserve the right to life, especially where a risk to life is apparent.

Therefore, if employers actively allow staff to physically intervene on their own (through consent or connivance) and a death results that could have been prevented by having the appropriate staffing numbers in place, then the organisation can be prosecuted for a violation of Article 2(1).

HOUSE OF LORDS JUDGEMENT IN SAVAGE V SOUTH ESSEX PARTNERSHIP NHS FOUNDATION TRUST

In a judgement on the 10 December 2008, in the case of Savage v South Essex Partnership NHS Foundation Trust, the House of Lords has provided useful guidance on the nature and extent of the obligation under Article 2 (The Right to Life) in the provision of healthcare. The judgment by the House of Lords confirms that where a patient is detained under the Mental Health Act and there is a *"real and immediate risk of suicide"* the positive obligations of Article 2(1) include a requirement to take operational steps to prevent that harm.

During the proceedings Baroness Hale noted that: *"the authorities are under an obligation to protect the health of persons deprived of liberty"* and that does not mean simply an obligation to have systems in place to provide access to necessary healthcare, but an obligation to provide it.

Therefore, if we look at the implications of Baroness Hale's statement we can draw from it that any 'authority' (or agents acting on behalf of any authority) who are empowered to intentionally remove the liberty of another individual are legally obliged to protect the health of the person whose liberty has been removed.

This means actually having systems in place to ensure that the risk is adequately assessed by suitably qualified individuals and that suitable and sufficient risk control measures are put in place (including the provision of adequately qualified and / or competently trained staff) to either eliminate the risk at source or, if that is not possible, reduce it to it's lowest possible level.

HOW OFTEN SHOULD RESTRAINT TRAINING BE REFRESHED?

There is no set time limit laid down by any Government statute or Associated Regulations, as to what would and what would not constitute a reasonable time period between initial training and subsequent refresher training in physical intervention.

However, it is good sense to refresh any physical skills being taught to staff on a regular and frequent basis if we are expecting staff to use such skills competently in their operational role. It would be naive to propose that a person trained in a system of restraint would maintain a suitably sufficient degree of competence without the ability to have their skills monitored and reviewed on a regular basis. In contrast it would be wise to assume that failure to refresh such skills can only lead to a degradation of skills in this activity and as such increase the margin of error and the risk of foreseeable injury.

By failing to refresh training skills on a regular basis, an employer may also be in breach of the Health and Safety at Work Act 1974. An employer may be failing in its duty of care to it's employees and others who may be affected by their acts and omissions, leaving itself open to a Criminal Offence and/or civil negligence. This is a view also echoed by other agencies.

In a finding by the Police Complaints Authority in their report *'Striking the Balance - The Police Use of New Batons'* it was identified that there was a relationship between the frequency of refresher training and the level of complaints. They found a reverse correlation between the frequency and extent of training and the number of complaints received. It stated: *"The more frequent the refresher training the lower level of such complaints."* In the report's recommendations, it states that the frequency of refresher training be reconsidered in the light of it's report.

Although the report was focused on the use of the new style Police batons, its findings should not be restricted solely to baton training. What we need to draw from this report is the inference that any system of skill training involving a degree of technical complexity and designed for use in operational situations where fear and anxiety will be present, should be regularly refreshed to reduce the risk of human error.

Her Majesty's Inspector of Constabulary highlighted the importance of refresher training in a report on Officer Safety Training in 1997. In the report (Office Safety – Minimising the Risk of Violence) it states; *"There are implications for forces and officers where refresher training is not undertaken within the set time limits, or where it is inadequately administered; an officer whose time limit has expired may not only breach force instructions but could be liable for civil negligence."*

In any physical intervention training package, that requires a level of technical knowledge, it must be accepted that the goals that are to be achieved in training will be less achievable in reality. This is due to the added pressures when a trained individual is faced with the reality of a violent assault. For example, goals, which may be achievable 70% of the time in training, may only be achievable 40% of the time in reality, due to added pressures.

Therefore, if we are to ensure continual competency in a person, who is expected to use physical intervention in their occupational role, we must accept that the skills they are initially trained in are perishable skills that will deteriorate with time. These skills will require refreshing to maintain a competent standard of operational skill, especially if the skills initially taught are to be used in situations that may increase the user's anxiety state due to the threat of physical violence.

In addition, many employed staff will be expected to use their discretion in situations where the use of physical intervention is used. To improve an individual's judgement we need to improve their knowledge and refresher training is an important component in the continual development of an individual's operational knowledge base, from which their discretion will be derived.

On this basis, the employer has a duty to ensure that there are appropriate arrangements in place for the planning, organisation, control, monitoring and review of the preventative and protective measures in place. This includes setting standards to judge performance, ensuring adequate supervision, making adequate routine inspections and checks etc.

Regulation 13 'Capabilities and Training' of the Management Regulations require employers to train their staff adequately when recruited; or when exposed to new or increased risks because of a transfer of workplace; or being given a change of responsibility; the introduction of a new system of work or a change in a system of work already within the employers undertaking. The 'Approved Code of Practice' (ACOP) states that:

> *"Employers should review their employee's capabilities to carry out their work, as necessary. If additional training, including refresher training, is needed, it should be applied."*

Any organisation therefore, that initially trains it's staff, has accepted that the training is required because a risk has been identified and the training has been implemented as part of an operational control measure. Therefore, as part of a continual training strategy the initial skills taught should be refreshed at regular periods to ensure continual operational competency of staff and compliance with the law. It would be very shortsighted not to do so, leaving the company increasingly liable for any injuries sustained by the activity as time passes.

In conclusion, the responsibility for restraint refresher training rests with the employer who is responsible for ensuring that employed staff are competent at what they are expected to do as part of their employed role. As such, it is for the employer to determine the frequency and duration of any refresher training as part of their process of risk management, and that decision should not be solely based on financial restrictions alone.

CHAPTER ELEVEN
THE CHARACTERISTICS OF SKILL PERFORMANCE

When we train staff in the use of physical intervention, it is important that the training provided can achieve the desired outcome, i.e., the physical control of an individual with minimal risk to all concerned. Therefore, it is fundamentally important that the physical skills taught to staff complement their ability to achieve the desired effect. This is also important if you consider the ergonomic approach to designing safe and effective physical intervention programmes and systems of work, as discussed in the previous chapter in Health and Safety.

To do this, we need to have an understanding of motor skills.

Motor skills can be defined as movements that are performed with a desired goal in mind. In sporting environments this may mean achieving such aims as holding a handstand in gymnastics. In physical intervention, it means being able to get staff to achieve the overall aim of controlling another individual in a safe, yet effective, way consistent with good practice and with minimal risk to all concerned.

To do this, we need to balance the ability of the staff, with the expectations of what they are required to do.

ABILITY

When we refer to ability, we draw reference to stable and enduring traits that for the most part, are genetically determined and underlie an individual's performance. Abilities range from visual activity to body configuration (height, weight and build); numeric ability; reaction speed; manual dexterity; kinesthetic sensitivity, etc.

There is also the difference in gender to consider. This is an important factor if the training is to be provided to a predominantly female workforce for example, who are expected to physically control males, as is the case in many care home settings. Recent research has highlighted this fundamental difference between men and women and although men and women should be equal in terms of their rights of equality and opportunity, men and women are definitely not identical in their innate abilities. There are fundamental differences that, if not addressed in a competent training package, will only serve to increase the risk to all concerned.

For example, the Allied Dunbar National Fitness Survey found that men are generally taller and heavier than women and that men have more active muscle tissue and an increased blood volume than females, contributing to them being faster, stronger, more powerful and having greater endurance.

A summary of some of the findings from the survey are itemised below:

- Men and Women have the same number of muscle fibres. However, the muscle fibres in men tend to be larger and this is thought to be linked to the male hormone testosterone. As a result, men tend to be stronger and more powerful than women because they have a greater lean muscle mass.

- Men have 10% larger hearts than women therefore having a greater capacity to pump more blood and oxygen around the body to feed the increased muscle mass.

- Men have 10% larger lungs than women resulting in a greater capacity to oxygenate the increased blood more effectively.

- Men also have 1 to 1.5 litres of blood more than women and within the blood, men have approximately 5.4 million blood cells per microlitre of blood whilst women have 4.8 million red blood cells per microlitre of blood. This means that men have a greater capacity for carrying oxygen in their blood than their female counterparts.

- Women also carry 10% more of their overall weight as fat than males. Therefore, the female heart has to work harder in order to deliver the same amount of oxygen to working muscles in a given time interval, resulting in men having more active muscle tissue than females, contributing to them being faster, stronger, more powerful, having higher aerobic and anaerobic power and greater endurance, than the average female.

What this research shows is that the physical and physiological differences between the sexes means that men have disproportionate levels of strength, power and endurance than females do.

In the context of undertaking physical intervention this means that men will be able to rely on greater reserves of strength, power and endurance during a physical conflict situation. On that basis, women who will be expected to use physical intervention, will require more effective methods of control, especially if they are expected to control a male who, by contrast, should be able to use lesser force and as such more appropriate (or non-harmful) methods to control a woman.

SKILL

To be skilled in the actual activity of physical intervention we must first define what we actually mean by "skill". To do this we need to turn to the definition of skill proposed by the psychologist E.R. Guthrie (1952), which captures three of the essential features of skilled behaviour. According to Guthrie, skill *"consists of the ability to bring about some end result with maximum certainty and minimum outlay of energy, or of time and energy."*

Individuals who are more proficient in achieving a particular movement goal usually demonstrate one or more of the following qualities mentioned in Guthrie's definition:

1. Maximum certainty,

2. Minimum energy expenditure, and

3. Minimum movement time

Therefore, if we are to train individuals to be competent in the activity of effecting physical intervention in a competent manner, whilst reducing the risks associated with manual handling and positional asphyxiation, achieving the three proficiencies is paramount.

These basic fundamental principles of skill criteria are so important that I have decided to cover them in more detail below.

1. MAXIMUM CERTAINTY OF GOAL ACHIEVEMENT.

To be "skilled" in any technique implies that a person is able to meet the performance goal, or "end result", with "maximum certainty". Only those individuals, who can produce the desired result with a high degree of certainty, on demand, without luck playing a very large role, can be considered skilled or competent.

For example, it is no good teaching a skill, that individuals cannot readily apply competently, in situations of high emotional arousal. If this is the case then the skill being taught will have a high degree of failure.

This is a fundamental principle to follow for all personnel expected to use physical intervention skills. By the very nature of its use (if it is to be used lawfully) physical intervention should only ideally be used as a last resort and therefore, by default, highly likely to be applied in situations that have escalated into ones of high emotional arousal, where a degree of risk is ever apparent.

However, if the staff required to do the intervening do not have faith in their system, or fear that the techniques they are trained in will not achieve the desired goal, it can lead to:

- Staff engaging prematurely to gain the advantage when dialogue and diversion would have been possibly more appropriate; and / or

- Staff not engaging when required to, due to fear of being disciplined, therefore allowing a greater harm to manifest itself to clients / service users;

Therefore, when designing a physical intervention skills training package it is important to ensure that the skills and technique taught in training, work in reality. This means that overly complicated techniques, that require a high degree of physical dexterity and cognitive complexity, should be removed or replaced with skills and techniques that are easier to learn, remember and recall. In addition, physical intervention systems should include as few techniques as possible, as opposed to teaching staff a wide and diverse range of technique options.

This fact seemed to be proved in a Report by Her Majesty's Inspectorate of Constabulary in 1997, regarding Officer Safety Training, which stated:

> *"A common complaint during the Inspection was that officer safety training, particularly in the use of certain batons, was overly complicated, requiring an excessive number of techniques...*
> *Most officers think they will not be able to remember the various techniques in confrontation situations and have*

forgotten them by the time they attend refresher train-
ing. A study in one force has disclosed that up to 80% of
officers assaulted during the period did not make use of
self-defence techniques to defend themselves, despite
being trained to do so."

2. MINIMUM ENERGY EXPENDITURE

The second quality of skill proficiency as defined by Guthrie, is the minimisation and conservation of the energy required for the action. This means the reduction or elimination of unwanted or unnecessary movement. This characteristic is crucial for those individuals who must conserve energy to achieve success.

If we apply this quality to the activity of physical intervention, we can see the relationship. Many people who may be expected to use physical intervention may not be motivated to use the skill. They may have joined their respective organisations for caring or other personal reasons and although they are probably (and hopefully) competent and proficient in their professional abilities, they may be at the lower end of the skill spectrum when it comes to the activity of physical intervention. Therefore, it is imperative that in teaching physical intervention to such individuals or employed groups that we construct programmes that do not require a high degree of energy or mental consideration in its application.

In addition, there will be staff who will be at the lower end of the fitness spectrum, or who are carrying injuries and are not likely to have the aerobic capacity to physically intervene for extended periods of time. In fact, they are likely to reach oxygen deficit between two to twelve seconds. After that they become exhausted and fatigue sets in. When this happens their ability is reduced, the holds become less effective and the margin for error increases which can lead to not only an increased risk of harm to the staff and service user, but also an increased risk of death as was highlighted in a Police Complaints Authority document *(Policing Acute Behavioural Disturbance - Revised Edition, March 2002)* which stated:

"The amount of time that restraint is applied is as impor-
tant as the form of restraint and the position of the de-
tainee. Prolonged restraint and prolonged struggling will
result in exhaustion, possibly without subjective aware-
ness of this, which can result in sudden death."

This is why it is important to reduce the amount of time that it takes to bring someone under control and in doing so, minimising any unnecessary energy expenditure.

3. MINIMUM MOVEMENT TIME

A third quality of skill proficiency is the reduced time (or increased speed) in which the goal is achieved. Skilled individuals are more effective when they execute their movements more quickly, such as the quick jab of the boxer.

However, if minimising time is achieved through speeding up a task by speeding up the movements within the task, then problems can occur. For example, a typist who speeds up the production of keystrokes on a computer may produce more errors in word processing, and a farmer who attempts to increase the speed of stacking hay bales in a barn may burn more energy.

This again, is an important quality to consider when designing physical intervention training programmes for operational use. Speed, in relation to the amount of time it takes, is an essential benefit in achieving control. However, speed should not be a component of a system that has been built in to compensate for a system that has too many techniques in it or which incorporate techniques requiring lots of multi-movements to make them work.

There has been a lot of research in recent years about the relationship between motor skills and performance, especially how certain skills respond when used in situations of distress or high pressure and the findings are very important in relation to physical intervention.

To understand this a little better, let's firstly define what a 'Gross' and a 'Fine' motor skill are.

A fine motor skill is one that is performed by the smaller muscles in the body such as the hands of fingers and which involve good hand-eye co-ordination. Activities such as playing the piano, handwriting or typing would be considered fine motor skills. Fine motor skills work best and achieve optimal performance in situations of low arousal. For example, if a concert pianist is about to walk on stage at the Royal Albert Hall the audience will be hushed to allow the pianist to concentrate on the complexity of what he or she is about to perform, and in many hospitals now classical music is played in the operating theatre to reduce the arousal of a surgeon about to undertake brain surgery on a sedated patient.

Gross motor skills on the other hand are skills that generally involve the actions of the larger muscle groups. Examples of gross-motor activity would be walking, running, pushing and / or pulling movements. Gross motor skills are also referred to as 'strength events' because it normally occurs in situations where a high level of arousal is taking place, which serves to increase the optimal performance level of the gross motor skill being used.

Therefore, if we are going to prepare people to physically intervene to control a person, who is out of control and exhibiting violence and aggression, in situations of possible fear and high emotional arousal, then staff should be trained in techniques that involve gross motor-skill construction if they are to be effective in what they do. Especially, if they are at the lower end of the ability / skill spectrum and / or fitness spectrum and as such do not have the aerobic capacity for a prolonged intervention.

Training someone in techniques that involve 'fine' or more 'complex' motor skill construction will only work if they are to be used in situations of low or non-existent stress. However, if the person is expected to use fine or complex techniques in situations of high emotional arousal then the technique is very likely to fail and the margin for error for an injury or a fatality to occur increases.

An appropriate and effective physical intervention system therefore needs to incorporate large major motor skills movements, comprising minimal construction within its technique syllabus and not compounded multi-move techniques, requiring minor motor skills movements.

Should there be a requirement for systems of physical intervention to be delivered, that require more techniques or movements, then consideration has to be given to the ability of staff to be able to achieve the skills within such a system; the amount of time spent on providing instruction to allow staff to become competent in use of the skills; and more regular refresher training to ensure that the skills are remembered.

WHY 'OFF THE SHELF' TRAINING FAILS

As a result, of all you have read, you can now see why many 'off the shelf' - 'one-size fits all' type of training packages fail and this was something that was also highlighted by Lady Nuala O'Loan in the case of Jimmy Mubenga who collapsed and died after being restrained by security guards on a BA flight out of Heathrow on the 12th October 2010.

Lady Nuala O'Loan also however, expressed her criticism about *"inadequate management of the use of force by the private sector companies"*.

In an interview in the Guardian newspaper she said that: *"There wasn't the management and there wasn't the training of guards"*. She felt that there was an urgent need to review the systems of physical intervention and went on to comment that: *"the training was textbook training but... it was one-size fits all: it made no difference whether they were dealing with a five foot girl or a 20 stone man"*.

Once again, this raises the issue and the need for you to do your own due diligence and not simply adopt a training package, purely on the basis that it is a "National Standard", which, if you consider the words of Lady Nuala O'Loan above, means that you may be adopting an 'off the shelf' - 'one-size fits all' training package, that may not be suitable for your organisation's specific needs.

Any training that you choose to implement or undertake must be fit for purpose as a suitable and sufficient control measure, and to do that it needs to meet the specific needs of your organisation, and it is your responsibility to ensure that it is.

Therefore, if anyone is offering you training and tells you that what they are offering you is a 'Nationally Recognised Standard' that meets your specific needs, then simply ask to see their risk assessments.

CHAPTER TWELVE
WHY HUMAN ERRORS REALLY OCCUR

*"Prime responsibility for accident and ill health preven-
tion, rests with management.*

*Accidents, ill health and incidents are seldom, random
events. They generally arise from failures of control and
involve multiple contributory elements. The immediate
cause may be a human or technical failure, but they
usually arise from organisational failings which are the
responsibility of management."*

HSG 65 – Successful Health and Safety Management

Over the last 30 years, we have learned a lot about the origins of
human failure. As a result, we can now formerly challenge, within a
structured Health and Safety Executive investigation model (HSG
48), the commonly held belief that incidents and accidents are simply and solely the result of 'human error' by the worker themselves.

Sadly however, attributing the blame for the accident as 'human
error' has for many years been 'convenient' for many organisations
and also many training providers. Why? - Simply because they can
provide unsafe systems of work or inadequate training and then
just blame any failing on the individual member of staff, with statements such as: *"If you had applied the technique properly it would
have worked".*

This does not mean that people do not cause or contribute to
accidents, but people are often set up to fail by the way our brain

processes information; by the training we are given; through the design of equipment and procedures and even through the culture of the organisation people work for, and these are identified in HSG 48 as 'latent failures'.

Latent failures are made by people whose tasks are removed in time and space from operational activities, as opposed to 'active failures' that are usually made by front line staff. Examples of the types of people involved in latent failures therefore could be: trainers, decision makers and managers and typically involve failures in health and safety management systems (design, implementation, monitoring and supervision).

In terms of physical intervention, an 'active failure' could be a member of staff who failed to implement a technique properly, which resulted in a service user or another member of staff being injured or killed. Latent failures however, that underpin the active failure, could be that the technique had a high degree of failure built in and was therefore highly unlikely to work in such situations; the staff were poorly trained and given incorrect information and instruction; and the company policy is legally flawed and has created uncertainty in what the staff can or cannot do when using physical intervention. These latent failures can result in staff operating from a position of fear and anxiety, as opposed to being operationally competent, which in turn increase the margin for error by creating an opportunity for an active failure to occur.

According to HSG 48: *"Latent failures provide as great, if not a greater, potential for danger to health and safety as active failures. Latent failures are usually hidden within an organisation until they are triggered by an event likely to have serious consequences"*.

In virtually every case, if a proper investigation is carried out, these latent failures are uncovered that will probably admonish the individual of any blame for the error and place the failing at the feet of the organisational management systems that have contributed to the failure.

In designing our courses, we have looked deeply into our responsibility in preparing individuals for what they are being trained to do, we have looked at the foreseeable human errors that could occur as a result of latent failings and then either eliminated them or reduced the likelihood of them occurring, which is what good health and safety risk management requires.

The HSG 48 model identifies two different types of human failures, which are: 'Errors' and 'Violations' (See Fig 1 below for details).

FIG 1: CAUSES OF HUMAN FAILURE HSG (48)

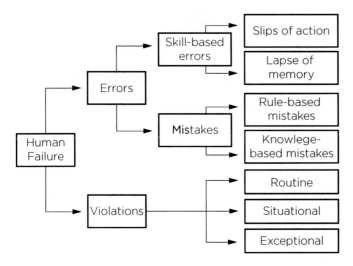

Let us start by firstly understanding 'Errors' and then look into what 'Violations' are later on.

ERRORS

Errors normally occur when an action or a decision was made that was not intended, involving a deviation from an accepted standard, which led to an undesirable outcome.

As you can see from the diagram, Errors fall into two main categories: skill based errors and mistakes.

Skill based errors are normally errors that occur in relation to the skill being undertaken or the technique being used and are therefore what we referred to earlier as 'direct failures'. As such they are normally directly associated with the actions of the person doing the skill or technique who normally gets blamed when it goes wrong.

However, 'skill based errors' can be broken down further into two sub categories which are: 'slips of action' and 'lapses of memory' which give us a more in-depth insight into why these errors actually occur and what we can do to minimise them.

SLIPS OF ACTION

'Slips of action' are failures in carrying out the actions of a task. They are described as 'actions-not-as-planned'. In general working conditions these could be: making a numerical or spelling mistake when copying written material; operating the wrong switch or turning a control the wrong way; and missing a step out of a sequence of a task.

Examples in a physical intervention programme would be:

- Using a different technique to the one the individual has been trained to do;

- Engaging in physical intervention too early or too late;

- Executing a technique with too much or too little strength;

- Holding a limb the wrong way.

LAPSES OF MEMORY

'Lapses of memory' cause us to forget to carry out an action, to lose our place in a task or even to forget what we had intended to do. They can generally be avoided by minimising distractions and interruptions to tasks and by providing effective reminders, especially for tasks that take some time to complete.

Examples that could create lapses in a physical intervention programme could be:

- Very finite or complex instruction from trainers;

- A programme that relies on too many techniques;

- Techniques made up of fine or complex motor skills or,

- A complex strategic structure, such as differing levels of control that involve different techniques: Level 1, Level 2, Level 3, etc.

All of the above can result in an inability, for staff being trained, to remember any instruction given or to be able to recall any physical techniques, if too many are provided or if they are made up of fine or complex motor skills.

Slips of action and lapses of memory can all be minimised in a good physical intervention programme by:

- Limiting the number of techniques that staff are expected to remember;

- Developing techniques that use gross motor skills and not fine or complex skills, and

- Using dynamic or pressurised training to prepare staff for the reality of the situations that they will be expected to intervene in.

Also, so that trainers do not lose themselves in the process the implementation of a simple 'audit checklist' that enables trainers to follow a pre-prescribed order and sequence of instruction would be a useful tool. Simply ticking off, what they have taught, as they go, would enable them to ensure that they have covered everything within the programme. This is also a highly valuable evidence tool if an individual came back to you at some time in the future and claimed that they hadn't been taught something that they should have been.

MISTAKES

Another reason an error occurs is when we make a mistake, and a mistake is when we generally do something wrong believing it to be right. As you can see by referring to the model in Fig 1, mistakes can be sub-divided into two sub-categories which are: 'rule-based mistakes' and 'knowledge-based mistakes'.

As with skill-based errors, mistakes are also generally attributed to the skill being undertaken or the technique being used and as such the person who used the skill or technique is normally blamed when things go wrong for "making the mistake". However, explore this concept a bit further and you will normally find that these 'mistakes' are possibly attributable to other factors (latent failures) and these will be explored here in the form of 'rule-based' and 'knowledge-based' mistakes.

'RULE-BASED' MISTAKES

A 'rule-based mistake' is where a 'rule' (or rules) exist that, generally speaking, have no basis in fact. In short, they have simply been made up by someone, without proper consultation or reference to, for example, any legal standard or understanding of the risks involved.

For example, an organisation or a training provider may have a 'rule' that says that a member of staff may not use a more restrictive intervention when controlling a violent person. However, when a non-restrictive technique is used and fails, and someone is injured, the member of staff may be blamed for 'making a mistake' by 'not doing the technique properly'. This would be an example of a 'rule-based mistake' (also a latent failure) that caused the more direct failure (the technique not working), which ultimately led to the error occurring.

Another example of a 'rule-based' mistake (or latent failure) that can lead to an error is when people in positions of influence use subjective opinion to come to a conclusion without any basis in fact; any specific training in that area; or any degree of operational competence in the subject matter they are commenting on. These people could include an organisational manager, a NVQ Assessor or a Government inspector, making comments or recommendations regarding the use of physical intervention, when they themselves are not trained or do not have any operational competence in that area.

If you remember, we wrote to the CSCI on the 12th September 2005 to ascertain what competencies or knowledge inspectors have in relation to physical restraint.

The reply we got stated:

> *"Starting with your final question, inspectors observations about the use of restraint will be based on the regulations and standards and other relevant documents such as the United Nations Convention on the Rights of the Child. Whether or not an inspector has received training in the use of physical restraint, will depend very much on his or her own past experience and training. Such training is not part of the required training for inspectors."*

So, if an untrained inspector on a visit to a care home or school started making subjective recommendations on the use of physical intervention, that, for instance, would be an example of a rule-based mistake, if those recommendations were then implemented and led to a restraint related failure.

'KNOWLEDGE-BASED' MISTAKES

Another form of 'mistake' is what is defined as a 'knowledge-based mistake'.

Knowledge-based mistakes typically occur when organisations rely on certain or specific individuals who are experienced and trained. What happens is that the information passed on by these individuals is sometimes relied upon too heavily and is rarely challenged, so it is not properly checked for accuracy.

One example of a 'knowledge-based mistake' could be, the trainer who uses their authority to tell people things that they themselves have been told to pass on, possibly based on incompetent rules. Sometimes the rules are even made up by the people with the experience and training, who may impose their authority on the people they are training so that what they say isn't questioned.

An example of how a knowledge-based mistake can arise in the field of physical intervention is when too much reliance is put on a member of staff who may be an ex-police officer or an ex-prison officer, and who the organisation presumes knows about physical intervention, simply because of the fact that they were once employed in those fields. As a result, they are given the responsibility, in some instances, even without any further training.

VIOLATIONS

Violations are a different animal altogether. They are any deliberate deviation from the rules, procedures, instruction and regulations. The breaching or violating of health and safety rules or procedures is a significant cause of many accidents and injuries at work.

However, violations are not normally driven by a desire to be subversive or to act with blatant disregard for health and safety. They are normally driven, and sometimes even encouraged (by consent or connivance), by other organisational factors and can be broken down into three sub-categories, which are: routine violations, situational violations and exceptional violations.

ROUTINE VIOLATIONS

Routine violations occur where breaking the rule has become the normal way of working within an organisation and one that is possibly, never challenged.

Routine violations can be due to:

- The desire to cut corners to save time.

- The perception that the rules are too restrictive.

- The belief that the rules no longer apply.

- Lack of enforcement of the rule, and

- New workers starting a job, where routine violations are the norm and they do not realise that this is not the correct way of working.

If you have ever heard the words: *"now forget what you've learned, this is the way we do it here"*, you will have just experienced a routine violation.

Routine violations can be minimised by:

- Identifying any unnecessary rules and getting rid of them.

- Implementing suitable and sufficient supervision and monitoring;

- Improving programme design that will reduce the need for staff to break the rules by removing processes, skills and techniques that do not work and by giving them the process, skills and techniques that work.

- Involve front-line staff in drawing up rules that affect how they are expected to operate.

SITUATIONAL VIOLATIONS

There are also 'situational violations' where breaking the rules is due to pressures from the job such as.

- Insufficient staffing levels:

- Lack of budget planning, and

- Staff being placed under unnecessary pressure. For example, many agencies advise staff not to restrain on their own but place them in situations where they are on their own, so inevitably staff violate the rules due to pressures of the situations they find themselves in.

EXCEPTIONAL VIOLATIONS

Exceptional violations occur when staff will break the rules even when they know that they are taking a potentially high risk because they believe that the benefits outweigh the risk.

For example, they will attempt to restrain someone who may have a knife because of the organisational and culture of the environment they work in which, although not condoned by management is not actively discouraged either. And this can be compounded even further, by staff who genuinely fear that if they don't take such risks, they could lose their job.

WHAT CAN YOU DO?

The old view of attributing accidents and injuries to human error alone, as a failing in the individual, is simply not good enough and can no longer be acceptable in today's society. All responsible organisations need to consider human factors as a distinct element, which must be recognised, assessed and managed effectively, if they are to provide physical intervention programmes that reduce the risk of injury and fatality.

In addition, all senior managers responsible for the training and development of their staff and for the commissioning of physical intervention programmes within their place of work should, as a bare minimum, undertake the training themselves, so that they can at least experience and understand first hand, what their staff are expected to do.

It is also vitally imperative that training providers understand what underpins human error and how these can be minimised through good programme design and delivery, so that the skill fits the individual, instead of trying to make the individual fit the skill. This requires an understanding of all aspects of not only skill instruction, but an understanding of the law, ergonomics, and even systems of dynamics, of relationships between people and inevitably, some understanding of psychology, especially the psychology of how people react under threat.

To download a full copy of HSG 48, go to the Health and Safety Executives website at:

www.hse.gov.uk/pubns/books/hsg48.htm

ENDNOTE

In conclusion, I would like you to consider the difference between logic and art.

Logic is reasoning, conducted or assessed according to strict principles of validity. Logic allows people to construct a valid, deductive, well calculated and thought out argument based on sound reasoning and fact, for the purpose of deciding a defensible outcome.

Art on the other hand is a creative skill. It allows individuals to produce imaginative designs and the expression of ideas through various art forms, such as painting and sculpture.

Logic is based on scientific principles, the first of which is to ensure that all assumptions should be identified and challenged.

Art on the other hand suspends these principles in favour of imaginative creativity.

Logic can be objectively assessed, whereas art relies on the perception of the individual. In short we all know that $2 + 2 = 4$, that is a logical calculation, but we can both look at a picture hanging in a gallery and have different opinions of how good or bad it is.

In the field of physical intervention, failure to use good logical reasoning to construct a practical and workable system of physical intervention, that is defensible by the very fact that it has been constructed around the rigorous discipline of a logical process, allows for artful subjectivity to creep in. It allows for ill-logical people, sometimes in positions of authority and influence, to express their imagination through creative subjective opinion.

However, as the famous quote from Sir Arthur Conan Doyle goes:

"When you have eliminated the impossible, whatever remains, however improbable, must be the truth."

To eliminate the impossible you must challenge all assumptions to find out if they are based on logical fact or whether they are merely the expression of someone's creative imagination.

This book has been written with the intention of providing you with the logic you need in order that you may move forward and use it as a means to help you create a practical defensible system of physical intervention that is legally, ethically and morally correct.

However, as I stated right at the beginning of this book, it is not an excuse for you not to do your own due diligence in this area, and I urge you to question everything, even this book. Take nothing for granted and do not assume anything.

Thank you for reading this and if you would like more information about who I am and what we do, please visit our website at:

www.nfps.info

MORE FROM NFPS

UNDERSTANDING REASONABLE FORCE AUDIO MP3 SET

These are not just a set of audio recordings. This is a culmination of over 22 years of work in Mark Dawes' professional field as one of the UK's leading Expert Witnesses in this area. Mark's research into all aspects and disciplines associated with his professional career have been honed not only operationally and in the classroom and gym, but also in Court and tribunals. The benefit to you in owning this unique set of recordings is that it will allow you to listen to them wherever you are in the world giving you the opportunity to upskill, re-train and remind yourself at your leisure.

For years we have prided ourselves with our mission of providing people with useful information and advice about what they can do as opposed to simply what they can't do. This set is a culmination of that mission. It is packed with information that is supported by the brilliant interviews with John Wadham, Gary Slapper and Michael Mansfield whose input alone is worth ten times the price of the set.

The Audio Recordings are possibly the most legally accurate set in existence and include:

- Introduction
- Use of Force and Health and Safety Legislation
- Understanding Reasonable Force
- The Use of Force with Children & Young People
- The Human Rights Act and the Positive Obligation to Preserve Life
- The Corporate Manslaughter & The Corporate Homicide Act 2007
- The Use of 'Pain-Compliance' Techniques and Their Legal Justification
- Reducing the Risk of Positional Asphyxia and Death due to Physical Restraint
- The Science and Psychology of Training & The Relationship between Motor Learning & Performance
- Interview With John Wadham
- Interview With Professor of Law Gary Slapper
- Interview With Michael Mansfield QC

For more information visit the web-site at:

www.nfps.info/reasonable-force-audio-mp3

LIVE THIS LIFE E-BOOK

I have written this book to help you change your life for the better, to help you make better choices and to help you find happiness in your life by the use of a positive mental attitude that will help you find true purpose in your life.

My aim in writing this book is to show you how phenomenal you really are and how you, as a human being, have the capability and resources inside of you to achieve extraordinary things. In this book you will learn more about your mind-body connection and how you can use that to its best effect to crate the changes you want in your life. For example, did you know that you have an internal dialogue of between 45,000 - 60,000 words a day? Simply becoming aware of that and changing some of your dialogue can have a massive effect on your life!

The book also looks at current research into what is called 'complex systems' and 'emergence' by Nobel-prize winning scientists that proves why exposure to fear, upset and conflict is vitally important for our brains to literally 'shift-gear' and move us towards a heightened sense of achievement that allows us to break through the barriers of limitation that holds so many of us back. What this means is that any unhappiness, upset or distress you are experiencing right now has a purpose, and that purpose is designed to take you to new heights of personal and professional achievement.

It also looks at why 'failure' may actually be a blessing in disguise and how some of the worlds greatest people were actually great failures before they ever became simply great!

In our current economic climate jobs are being lost everyday and many people are worrying about their future. If you are one of these people then this book is a must for you.

In our family lives many of us will be challenged by our children who themselves may be going through a difficult and hard time, and as a parent we may not know what to do or where to go to for advice. This book is for you.

You may be in a position in your life right now where you believe that you have lost everything and that you are to old or too inexperienced to start over again. This book is for you.

My aim in writing this book has been to give you a few key tools and concepts and a definitive strategy to help you change your life for the better, despite how you may be feeling and in-spite of your current emotional state and circumstances.

The Chapters of the E-Book are:

Chapter 1 - 50 Folds of Paper

Chapter 2 - You Are God-Like

Chapter 3 - Let's go down the mind gym

Chapter 4 - Your Unconscious 'Servo-Mechanism' to Success

Chapter 5 - The Mind as a Fertile Field

Chapter 6 - How to use Autosuggestion and Self-Talk

Chapter 7 - What Doesn't Kill us Makes us Stronger

Chapter 8 - Joining the Dots of Life - Steve Jobs' Speech

Chapter 9 - Failure – A Blessing in Disguise

The cost to Download this e-book is only £3.47 + vat at:

www.nfps.info/live-this-life

UNDERSTANDING REASONABLE FORCE BOOK BY MARK DAWES

Mention the words 'Reasonable Force' and you come up with a recipe that evokes heated debate among many. The case of the Norfolk farmer, Tony Martin for example, was seen by many as a travesty of justice, but the upside of the case was the first time, virtually every person in the UK started asking: 'What does "Reasonable Force" actually mean? There is lots of subjective advice dished out by well meaning individuals as to what they think Reasonable Force means, and many law-abiding citizens accept this advice, sometimes without question. However, much of the advice given is negative in it's content. It tells us what we can't do – not necessarily what we can.

This book is different. It is about what we can do. It's about re-dressing the balance. It is about what our rights are, especially the right, and indeed at times duty, to use Reasonable Force. This is a right granted to us by statute, enshrined by our common law and enforced by Human Rights legislation. This book explores that right fully. It is a liberating book that informs us of our rights and tells us what we can do as opposed to purely what we can't, which is consistent with the state of mind all human beings need to possess if they are to function responsively in a democratic society. To purchase the book go to:

www.nfps.info/Products

PHYSICAL INTERVENTION INSTRUCTORS QUALIFYING COURSE

The main aim of the Course is to qualify you with a BTEC Level 3 Advanced Award in Physical Restraint Instruction making you a professionally qualified Physical Restraint / Physical Intervention Instructor.

The cost of the course is fully inclusive and includes: accommodation and meals at Lilleshall National Sports Centre, Comprehensive Instructors Manual, Audio MP3 Recordings, 8 x Powerpoint Presentations, 2 x e-books, Risk Assessments (included in the manual), BTEC Certification & NFPS Accreditation Certification.

We also provide you with sample templates and course documentation to enable you to run your own courses on immediate completion of the trainers course!

If you are interested in becoming a Physical Intervention Trainer then visit our web-site at: For other products please visit NFPS Ltd's web-page at:

nfps.info/NFPS-BTEC-Level-3-Restraint-and-Breakaway-Instructors-Course

UNDERSTANDING QUANTUM THINKING BOOK

This book looks at the way we think and how our thoughts affects our health, wealth and relationships. It explores how we can adopt new principles that will lead us towards adopting a more functional way of thinking and as such, a more functional way of living. This book has been a catalyst for change for many people and has received 10 Five star reviews on Amazon.co.uk.

Think about it, How would life be different for you if you suddenly found that you had the power to create abundance in any area of your life? What would you do differently now if you knew that you had the ability to tap into the infinite realm of possibilities that could change your life forever? Quantum Thinking has already changed many people's lives for the better. It has released many individuals from the shackles of negativity that imprison them within their own minds and set them free to explore and experience the infinite universe of possibilities that awaits everyone of us.

Are you ready to become the person you want to be-the one that already exists inside of you? To order your copy of the book go to:

www.nfps.info/Products

WHAT IS SELF DEFENCE DVD

This is a brand new information product packed with lots of information regarding your rights to self defence. In it Mark Dawes and Professor of Law Gary Slapper reveal exactly what you rights to self defence are and disclose information that some people won't tell you about and what others simply either don't know or don't want you to know.

For more information on this unique and specialised product, from two of the UK's leading experts, go to:

www.whatisselfdefence.com

FREE INFO

For lots of free info including news articles, industry and legal updates and advice on forthcoming courses sign up for our FREE e-mail newsletter by going to:

www.nfps.info/FreeInfo